D0815979

a sure Path

a sure Path

Moving Ahead with Christ When We'd
Rather Settle Down in the World

SUSAN SCOTT SUTTON

Kregel
Publications

*A Sure Path: Moving Ahead with Christ When We'd Rather
Settle Down in the World*

© 2003 by Susan Scott Sutton

Published by Kregel Publications, a division of Kregel, Inc., P.O.
Box 2607, Grand Rapids, MI 49501.

All rights reserved. No part of this book may be reproduced,
stored in a retrieval system, or transmitted in any form or by
any means—electronic, mechanical, photocopy, recording, or
otherwise—without written permission of the publisher, except for brief quotations in printed reviews.

Unless otherwise indicated, Scripture quotations are from the
Holy Bible, New International Version®. © 1973, 1978, 1984 by International Bible Society. Used by permission of Zondervan Publishing House. All rights reserved.

Scripture quotations marked ASV used by permission of Thomas
Nelson, Inc., original publisher of the *American Standard Version.*

Scripture quotations marked NASB are from the *New American
Standard Bible,* © the Lockman Foundation 1960, 1962, 1963,
1968, 1971, 1972, 1973, 1975, 1977.

Cover design: John M. Lucas

Library of Congress Cataloging-in-Publication Data
Sutton, Susan.
A sure path: moving ahead with Christ when we'd rather settle
down in the world / by Susan Scott Sutton.
    p. cm.
Includes bibliographical references.
    1. Christian life. I. Title.
BV4501.3 .S88   2003
348.4—dc21   2002152256

ISBN 0-8254-3661-3

Printed in the United States of America

03 04 05 06 07 / 5 4 3 2 1

To Louis,
who is with me on the journey
—Psalm 34:3

Contents

Acknowledgments 9

Introduction: A Letter to Young Pilgrims 11

1. The One Way Home 17
2. Hearts on Pilgrimage 31
3. A Companion for the Path 45
4. A Focus for the Path 61
5. A Light for the Path 73
6. A Path of Faith 89
7. A Path of Trust 103
8. A Path of Hope 117
9. A Path of Praise 131
10. A Path of Obedience 145
11. A Path of Glory 167
12. A Path That Leads Home 185

Conclusion: Reflections on Psalm 84
from a Wandering Pilgrim 195

Endnotes 199

Acknowledgments

Once again, heartfelt thanks to:

My "critics corner": Leslie Venable, Lisa Gramman, and Sheila Norris. This is the second time I have come home from Chad and thrown a manuscript your way for comments. Thank you for actually wanting to read through such unrefined pages and for encouraging me to keep going. Leslie, I especially thank you for your insights given so graciously. The hours spent at your house with cups of coffee or chai in hand discussing yet another book about God's truths gave a lot of shape to these pages. Sheila, it was your final look at these pages and willingness to go through it with me page by page one fine summer evening that saw it through to the end. Thanks so much.

Robby and Betsy Buck, as well as dear friends at Christ the King Moravian Church: you brought this book before the throne of our great God, knowing how much I wanted it to be fully His.

The staff at Kregel: Thank you for encouraging me by asking if I was writing another book. It so happened that I was, and here it is. Your confidence in my writing has encouraged me tremendously, and you have been great to work with.

My husband, Louis: this book is dedicated to you, and rightly so, because most of the examples from our travels in Chad are yours. The chapter on God's glory really should have your name on it. But even if I had not already decided to dedicate it to you, I would surely have done so at the end; it could never have been finished without your constant support and personal sacrifices. The final manuscript was written in the place where we spent a few weeks before heading back to Chad—a quaint unheated house in northern France located at the foot of a thirteenth-century castle. This sounds idyllic for a writer's retreat and it was, but only because of your commitment to my writing. You chopped the wood and built the fires in the woodstove and fireplace to keep us warm, shopped for all the food, cooked all the meals, and did all the laundry, so I was able to concentrate on finishing these pages. Thank you for showing me always what is a true example of a servant's heart.

Introduction

A Letter to Young Pilgrims

Two images have shaped my life of faith for many years: life as pilgrimage and faith as a walk with God. Both of these images reflect our years spent on earth as a journey and both are underlying threads that run throughout this book. Many times while writing these pages, I thought about our three children, Susan, Elizabeth, and Scott, who as emerging young adults are beginning in earnest their journeys of faith. I thought of how much their father and I long for them to live their lives as fully for the Lord as we have sought to do, and I realized that in a very real sense the book was being written for them. At some point in its early stages, I sat down and wrote a letter to let them know this and called it *A Letter to Young Pilgrims*. When the letter was finished, though, I put it aside as too personal for the book. They would read it on their own at some other time, perhaps as a note inserted in their personal copies of the book. But then I picked it up again later to reread. In doing so, I realized something else: that the hopes I expressed for them are the same hopes I have for anyone who might read this book—including you.

So I have decided to make the letter itself the introduction. I ask that as you read it you insert your own name in the opening line, and apart from the obviously personal references, take this letter as your own:

Dear Scott, Elizabeth, and Susan,

This book is dedicated to your father, and I have no doubt you can understand why. But it is written for you. In a few years you will be making your way in this world, more on your own than ever before. And it's an interesting world out there. Interesting in the sense of exciting, adventurous, lots to see and experience, full of surprises; but also interesting in the sense of "Hmmmm . . ." There will be much to make you ponder. And some of what you will ponder is the reality of your faith in Christ. The faith that you've taken on as a result of your life thus far (your heritage from Christian parents, surroundings on a mission field, etc.) will be challenged when you are no longer living under our roof and the surroundings change. When you step into the big world out there you enter an arena that continually questions the reality of what you now believe.

You have already acknowledged that God has no grandchildren, only children, and have each made your own decision to live for Him through Christ. Your father and I see you now growing in a personal faith. What you have is no longer borrowed from us; it has become your own. This is important, because what is your own will go with you wherever you are and in whatever you do in the years ahead. It will not be as easily set aside as something borrowed.

But it will be challenged. Your faith in God and in Christ as the only way to Him will be challenged from the outside when you increasingly meet people, lifestyles, and ideas that get along very well without such a faith. It will be challenged by many respected and intelligent people who simply do not believe it and quite happily say so. I think of the CNN interview on New Year's Eve 2000 with Sir Arthur Clarke. We were watching it together in Chad in the home of a friend who has a satellite dish. A young boy, and I admire him for his courage, asked Sir Arthur Clarke the ultimate question, "Do you believe in God?" Sir Clarke smiled graciously at the boy and replied, "No, I don't, but I don't disbelieve in her, either."

There you have it in a nutshell. Modern man quelling in one sentence both belief in God and traditional concepts of God.

Your faith will also be challenged by people who believe as sincerely as you believe, but in something else. It will be challenged by a world that doesn't want to be challenged by biblical truth and so will call you intolerant, perhaps even bigoted, because of your choice to follow Christ. Following Christ means taking Him seriously when He speaks of living to please God, and pleasing God means living by specific standards. You will find that these biblical standards don't always sit well next to the current mind-set that "anything goes."

Your faith will also be challenged from within. Only God knows what lies ahead for you. Your father and I, of course, would like your lives to be smooth, successful, full of joy, and essentially trouble free. But reality has to be faced. It just won't be so. We live in a world that is imperfect and scarred by sin. Simply by living, you will be touched by the consequences of an imperfect and scarred world. You have a firm foundation already laid, but the shape of what you build on this foundation, what you think of God, of life, and of yourselves, will be influenced by what you experience in the years ahead.

At this point you have chosen your path and begun the journey. It is the right choice. Your father and I know this. But the fact that we know it isn't enough, of course. As much as you respect our views, they certainly won't be enough to hold down the anchor of your faith in the inevitable gales of life that lie ahead. You need to know it for yourselves.

What you need to know is that the path you have chosen is the right path, not because we say so, but because God Himself says so. As you experience your personal journey of faith, He will prove this to you over and over again.

How you walk this path of faith in the years ahead will depend much on God, "being confident of this, that he who began a good work in you will carry it on to completion until the day of Christ Jesus" (Phil. 1:6) and much on yourselves, "urging you to live lives worthy of God, who calls you into his kingdom and glory" (1 Thess. 2:12). This book is to encourage you to do your part, to take your life with God as seriously as He does. It is to remind you that the life of faith is a journey; therefore, it is a walk along a path that heads toward a destination. And it is to remind you that the path you walk is a sure one; therefore, you can walk it with confidence no matter what and whom you meet along the way.

"You are not your own; you were bought at a price. Therefore honor God in your body" (1 Cor. 6:19–20), and in your mind and in your words and in your actions and in your choices and in your relationships, glorify God.

Your father and I pray that as you walk this certain path in an uncertain world, you will experience the joy of knowing God, of loving Him, and of serving Him in this world. There is no greater knowing, no deeper joy, no surer path.

All my love, Mom

In choosing to read this book, I assume that you, the reader, *are* taking your life with God as seriously as He does and that you want to grow in understanding of what it means to live life with and for Him. Wherever you are in your faith, whether a beginner with no knowledge of what lies ahead on the path or already a seasoned traveler, it is the path that concerns you now, and it is the path that I want to write about in this book. I hope that the pages ahead will provide some nourishment for the journey.

At the end of each chapter is a section called "Notes for the Journey," designed to take you to God's Word for personal study. Gloria Gaither once observed that "in our relationship with God there is much to be said and God is the one who must say it." We can enjoy very much the writings of others and they do carry us farther along in the faith, but in the end it is God who must have the final word. I hope that you will take time to study the verses suggested. God will speak to you through His Word on these subjects far better than I can write about them. Most of the studies are focused on a theme and some have quite a few verses to look up. You may want to read through the book first and then go back to the studies. Take your time with them and stretch each chapter study over several days to make sure that you're soaking in the beauty and truth of the Scriptures, not just looking up each verse to record an answer. None of the chapters exhaust their themes, so I also hope that each one will really be a springboard for you to do further study on your own.

Finally, in a way, by writing this book, I am bringing you along for a while on my own journey of faith. You will find as you read that I draw quite a bit from the well of our experiences as missionaries in Chad because these make up the main path, at least during the past twelve years, on which God has taught us so much of His faithfulness. If you find it hard to relate to some of these examples, I trust that you can relate to His truths, which are the same whether they are learned on the edge of the sub-Sahara or in the suburbs of Chicago.

The path ahead beckons. Come with me. Let's travel together for a while and see what God might have to say.

One

The One Way Home

There is no getting to heaven as our
home but by Christ as our way.
—Matthew Henry

And a highway will be there;
it will be called the Way of Holiness.
—Isaiah 35:8

On the road to Adre you feel as if you are heading for the ends of the earth. Our family has traveled this road innumerable times during the past twelve years of missionary service in Chad, so we know the feeling well. For six of those years we actually lived in Adre, which was then little more than a bush town on the border of Sudan, and so during these years the road to Adre for us meant the road to home. Whenever we traveled this road from the starting point of another town, we looked forward to the end point of arrival because friends, ministry, house, and almost every possession we could call our own waited for us at the other end. I have to admit, though, that we rarely looked forward to the journey.

You can understand why when you know the nature of the road we had to travel to get home. Leading in and out of Adre is a major east-west highway that stretches across Africa from Port Sudan to Douala, Cameroon, making this "highway" an important trade route, not to mention the only route for miles around. This sounds rather impressive until you are actually on the road itself. Then you find that the Chadian section of this major African highway is nothing but a fairly wide dirt path that narrows at intervals into a sand track for miles at a time.

Visitors who travel the road with us for the first time are incredulous that this uneven dirt path is actually a major highway. My husband, Louis, drives the road with familiar ease but still has to dodge potholes, skirt herds of goats and sheep, and brake full stop for the occasional donkey who has parked himself for a rest in the middle of our path, refusing to move for even large oncoming vehicles. We are convinced that this is the humble donkey's one defiant act to the world.

Endless hours of feeling like a milk shake in process make the journey seem extra long. In fact, due to the conditions of the road the journey does take longer than it should. The actual distance from a starting point of Abeche, a larger town to the west, is only 100 miles. In the United States such a journey on a major highway would take less than two hours. On a good day for traveling in Chad, during the dry season with the road in its best condition, the journey from Abeche to Adre takes four to five hours. During the rainy season when torrential showers turn the road into a mudslide and flowing rivers defy crossing, the journey can take from eight hours to two or three days.

You might well wonder if we ever ask ourselves if it's worth the trouble it takes to travel this road! But we never ask the question "Is it worth it?" Obviously we would prefer better conditions for travel. A smoother surface and fewer obstacles to slow us down along the way would be much appreciated. But home is in only one direction and there is only one road to take us there. So we pack up the car, pile the family and any Chadian passengers who may have asked for a ride in, and follow this one road no matter how difficult it may prove to be because we know this is the road that will lead us home.

And so it is for the Christian's journey of faith. As with any journey, our faith has a departure point and a point of arrival but what concerns us now is all that lies between, the one way we must travel to reach home.

This path never once promised to be smooth and bump-free, without steep inclines or stubborn obstacles in our way to slow us down, but we know it is the right one to travel so we keep going despite the conditions we might meet along the way.

Departure and Arrival

The life of faith has a point of departure with all of its hopes for the journey ahead. This point comes when we respond to Christ's call to follow Him. We have discovered that there is much more to life than we ever thought possible and this "much more" is found in Jesus, the Author of Life Himself. We say yes to all He has done for us, through His death on the cross, and yes to all He is for us, the resurrected Lord. We look forward with hope to all He will do in us and with us and through us as we begin a new life with Him. Like the apostle Paul, we do not want to remain where we are but we want to "press on toward the goal to win the prize for which God has called me heavenward in Christ Jesus" (Phil. 3:14).

Grace at the cross has opened the door and hope in the risen Christ now leads the way. What a starting point for the journey! No wonder we begin our life in Christ with such anticipation.

There is also a point of arrival. The farther we travel along the path of faith the greater the anticipation of reaching home and everything we have come to hold dear. The details of our destination may sometimes seem a bit vague (we can only imagine what heaven will truly be like, even with the Bible as a guide), but Scripture is clear that heaven is a real place and that God is there:

> Acknowledge and take to heart this day that the LORD is God in heaven above and on the earth below.
> —Deuteronomy 4:39

The LORD is in his holy temple;
the LORD is on his heavenly throne.
—Psalm 11:4

We also know that because we have put our faith in Christ we will be
with Him in heaven for eternity.

After this I looked and there before me was a great multitude
that no one could count, from every nation, tribe, people and
language, standing before the throne and in front of the Lamb.
—Revelation 7:9

And so we will be with the Lord forever.
—1 Thessalonians 4:17

"In my Father's house are many rooms," Jesus declared in the hours
before He was arrested. He then added as if to make sure we believe
Him, "If it were not so, I would have told you." Not only is there a place
for us in heaven, but Jesus Himself will prepare it for us and then will
come Himself to take us there.

I am going there to prepare a place for you. And if I go and prepare a place for you, I will come back and take you to be with
me that you also may be where I am.
—John 14:2–3

Heaven is not a myth or a hopeful idea. It is a place, and one day we
will be there. One day, but not yet. In the meantime, there is life to be
lived on earth and our faith to be shaped while we live it. There is all that
lies between the anticipation point of departure and the celebration point
of arrival. There is the one road to be traveled that will take us home.

The One Way Home

Our family knows that the long dirt road heading toward Adre is the only way to our home in Chad. It is this certainty that we are headed in the right direction that keeps us going even when there are difficulties along the way and even when others might challenge our sense of direction. As Christians we make a claim with equal certainty. Our claim is that Jesus is the one way to God and, therefore, the only way to eternity in heaven. Such a claim is becoming increasingly taboo in today's world, but even at the risk of being branded out-of-date, unsophisticated, or, as is becoming more and more the case, intolerant, Christians continue to say that there is one path to God that everyone, regardless of culture or background, must take to reach Him.

Sadly, there are an increasing number of people in churches today and even their pastors who are not willing to make this claim. Louis and I were recently in a Sunday School class that was discussing C. S. Lewis's *Mere Christianity.* The particular chapter for that Sunday discussion dealt with pride, and in the course of the class, someone stated that it is really prideful for Christians to say that Christ is the only way to God. A few eyebrows rose at this suggestion, but we were sad to see how many heads nodded in agreement.

It would indeed be prideful if we were the ones who originally said it. But we are not. God is the One who says it, and we are taking Him at His Word. What is prideful is when we presume to speak for God something other than He has spoken for Himself.

The Christian message is only that which God Himself has spoken: that He loves us very much, this world that He created, and that sin has blocked us from Him. That we could never hope to reach Him until our sin had been dealt with and that God, knowing this helplessness of ours to reach Him, reached out to us Himself in the person of His Son, Jesus Christ. Through Christ He dealt with sin once and for all. Through Christ the way is now open for us to know God, now on earth and for eternity.

Through His words and actions while on earth, Jesus proved Himself to be the presence of God among us. He spoke of Himself often as the way to God through images such as a gate, a shepherd, and bread, but He stated His identity openly in a conversation that is recorded in the gospel of John. Jesus was talking with the disciples about heaven and, as we have seen above, He spoke of preparing a place for them where He would be going and assured them that one day He would return to take them there. From our perspective we know exactly what Jesus was talking about, but the disciples were less enlightened, and so a confused Thomas asked how they could know the way to where He was going. Jesus answered Thomas with the words, "I am the way and the truth and the life. No one comes to the Father except through me" (John 14:6).

The disciples wanted to know the way to where He was going and Jesus told them. We learn as much from what Jesus did not say as from what He said. He did not say, "I know the way" or "There are many ways" or "Do these things and you will find the way." Jesus said, "I am the way. . . . No one comes to the Father except through me" (John 14:6). After Jesus' death on the cross, after His resurrection and return to heaven before their eyes, and after the coming of the Holy Spirit, the disciples were no longer confused. They fully understood who Jesus is and this became their message to the world:

> Salvation is found in no one else, for there is no other name under heaven given to men by which we must be saved.
> —Acts 4:12

The Christian message goes further. Not only did Christ dwell among us physically for thirty years on earth, but we are so bold as to claim that He continues to dwell with us even now two millennia later. We can make such a staggering claim because Jesus' life did not end at the cross. His physical death on the cross was merely the door to a resurrected body that never dies. The last words of Jesus that are recorded in the gospel of

Matthew are a promise reminiscent of God's promise to Moses in Exodus 33: "And surely I am with you always, to the very end of the age" (Matt. 28:20).

Ever since the creation of the world, humanity has reached out to God either through religious performance as in Islam or through denial of human nature as in the Eastern religions. Only Christianity claims that God came alongside of us as we are in our imperfect humanity and in doing so provided the way for us to be with Him forever.

"All roads lead to Rome" may have been true for a point in time for ancient civilizations, but it is not true for the eternal God who has a truth about Himself that He has revealed to the world. In His appointed time, the Word, God Himself, "became flesh and made his dwelling among us." As a result, "we have seen his glory, the glory of the One and Only, who came from the Father, full of grace and truth" (John 1:14).

A Lord to Follow

On the journey of faith, we have a departure point when we first became Christians, an arrival point when we reach our true home in heaven, and the path we travel following Jesus Christ as the one way to get there. But there is something else to say about our path. We will never make progress on it by standing still. Being on a journey automatically means movement.

When Jesus called the disciples to join Him, they did not respond with words but with movement. They got up from the boat and the table and went after Him. They had to move or else Jesus would have become just a figure walking away from them until He faded in the distance. If the disciples had remained where they were, think of what they would have missed. They would have missed rubbing shoulders with eternity. They would have missed being an active part of God's kingdom work. They would have missed a love, a joy, a peace, and a hope greater than any they had ever before known. They would have been left with a belief, true as it was, but there would have been no relationship with the true and living Son of God.

When Christ calls us to follow Him today, He means just that. We are to follow. His call to follow is a summons to be involved with Him personally, to come alongside of Him and be where He is. It is a call to relationship. Sadly, there are many Christians in the church today who don't know this. They have a genuine belief in Christ but no relationship with Him, so what they follow is more a set of rules, a particular doctrine, or perhaps simply a lifestyle that they find attractive, but not the person of Jesus Christ. Because they have not left where they are in order to be where Christ is, in their thinking, in their actions, in their priorities, goals, and ambitions, they have a Christian belief but are no farther along the path of faith than when they first entered church. In truth, they have more of a "churchianity" rather than Christianity, for there is no Christianity without Christ, and there is no Christ in our life without a response to His call to follow.

To follow means to go after. According to *Vine's Expository Dictionary of Old and New Testament Words,* the Greek verb used for all references to following Christ is *akaloutheo.*[1] The prefix *a* expressing union or likeness is joined with *keleuthos* meaning "way" to describe a follower: one who goes in the same way. Following means leaving my way in order to go the same way as someone or something else. Following Christ means leaving my way in order to go His way.

Some Questions for the Path

If you have responded to Christ's call to follow Him, then you are on the path of faith already and will be on it until that glorious moment when you meet the Lord face-to-face. I wonder what your path has been like? What have you encountered along the way? Has it been what you expected? If you were to publish a diary of your Christian life to this point, what would you choose for a title? Would your title reflect the lilting dance of Ingrid Trobisch's *On Our Way Rejoicing!*[2] or be closer to the steady march of *A Long Obedience in the Same Direction* by Eugene Peterson?[3] Both titles reflect essential truths of the journey.

If you understand that life with Christ is a journey headed toward a destination, do you know where you are headed? Do you recognize that this world is not your home and that you are just passing through it while heading to your true home in heaven? Does it matter to you?

It should matter a great deal. What we believe about heavenly realities affects how we live with earthly realities. It shapes our identity as we travel. It influences our choices along the way. It has a great deal to do with what we think of the path we find ourselves on as we follow Christ; whether or not we think that this path, with all of its twists and turns, its unexpected bumps and stubborn obstacles, its bleak landscape at times, is worth the effort it takes to keep going.

How are you feeling about your particular path at this point? Is it hard? Is it different from what you had expected? If you are serious about following Christ, the journey *will* be hard at times. Jesus asks everything of us when He calls us to deny ourselves, take up our cross daily, and come after Him (Luke 9:23). We do well to realize the seriousness of a positive response to following Him. But when we, like the disciples, get up from where we are and respond to Christ's call with a commitment to follow wherever He leads, we find that in return for asking all, He gives us all— all of Himself and all that we ever truly need for life.

Those who persevere on the path grow in their understanding of what it means to follow Christ. And as they follow, they experience His great faithfulness and learn to love Him more and more along the way. The question for true followers when the path becomes difficult is never "Is it worth it?" but "Is He worthy?" The answer to that question is always yes.

Notes for the Journey

We must seek the Savior. When He was on the earth, He invited men to company with Him; thus they came to know Him, and in knowing Him to know His Father.... The Lord Jesus Christ is now absent from us in body, but spiritually it makes no difference; still we may find and know God through seeking and finding His company. It is those who have sought the Lord Jesus till they have found Him—for the promise is that when we seek Him with all our hearts, we shall surely find Him—who can stand before the world to testify that they have known God.[4]

—J. I. Packer

For Reflection

How would you describe your Christian faith at this point? As "churchianity," having a belief in God and involvement in a church but little more, or Christianity, following Christ as Lord?

Read the verses below and write in your own words what Jesus says it means to follow Him:

- Matthew 10:37–39
- Luke 9:23–26
- Luke 14:25–27
- John 12:25–26

There were some who hesitated to follow Jesus for various reasons. Read these accounts and write in your own words why they hesitated.

- Luke 9:57–62
- Luke 18:18–27

Sometimes Jesus sounds harsh in His insistence on leaving family or wealth behind in order to follow Him. What does He really mean by this? Think about His words in light of these verses:

- Exodus 20:3–4
- Deuteronomy 6:4–5
- 1 John 2:15–17

How do these verses help us understand that Jesus is not giving a literal command for everyone to leave family, wealth, or vocation behind in order to follow Him but instead is talking about priorities and attitude of the heart?

- Mark 5:18–20
- Romans 14:3–5, 10, 23
- Ephesians 5:33–6:4
- 1 Timothy 6:17–19

At one point in Jesus' ministry, a large crowd of disciples decided to turn away from following Him because what He was teaching was too hard for them to accept. How did Peter respond when Jesus asked the twelve disciples if they would do the same?

- John 6:60–69

Suggestion

In my early years as a Christian I often heard the statement "Christ is either Lord of all or not Lord at all." From time to time I need to be reminded of this and ask the question: Is Christ Lord of all in my life? How about for you?

Make a list of the things that matter the most to you (loved ones, finances, resources, talents, time, dreams, hopes, house or car, for example). Go through the list one by one. Can you say of each one, "Christ is Lord of . . ."? What does it mean for you to say Christ is Lord in each situation? (For example: "Christ is Lord of my job." What does that mean? How does it change your attitude in your job if you truly have put it under the lordship of Christ? Or "Christ is Lord of my marriage." What does that mean? More trust? More commitment? More effort to make the home a Christ-centered home? More prayer together as husband and wife?)

Write a prayer of commitment in the areas that need to be submitted more fully to Christ's lordship.

This world is not conclusion;
A sequel stands beyond,
Invisible as music,
But positive, as sound.
It beckons and it baffles,
Philosophies don't know,
And through a riddle, at the last,
Sagacity must go.
To guess it puzzles scholars;
To gain it, men have shown
Contempt of generations,
And crucifixion known.

—Emily Dickinson

Two

Hearts on Pilgrimage

On earth we are wayfarers, always on the go ... keep on
walking, moving forward, trying for the goal.
—Augustine

Blessed are those whose strength is in you,
who have set their hearts on pilgrimage.
—Psalm 84:5

I f you make a trip to Israel to see the places where Jesus walked while
on earth, the tour guide might ask at some point, "Are you here as a
tourist or as a pilgrim?" Although the question sounds like a comment
against too many flashing cameras and chatty sightseers, the guide isn't
being critical. His reason for the question is to make the visit enjoyable
for everyone. He knows that the tourist and the pilgrim have come for
different reasons. The tourist's motivation is personal pleasure. The
pilgrim's motivation is worship. The tourist wants to see the sights, collect memories, and then move on. The pilgrim has come for something
deeper, more lasting. He wants to encounter God. So a tour guide who
asks this question will separate the tourists from the pilgrims in order
to satisfy each group. The tourist can then move around freely without
worrying about disturbing anyone else. Those who have come to encounter God can do so without distraction.

It's not a bad idea to ask the same question concerning our life of faith. Am I on this journey as a tourist or as a pilgrim? How I answer the question is important. It cuts to the root of my motivation for becoming a Christian and reveals whether walking with Christ, in my mind, is ultimately about me or about Him. There is absolutely nothing wrong with traveling as a tourist to the place where Jesus prayed in the Garden of Gethsemane, yet when it comes to our life with Christ we are to be on the journey not as tourists but as pilgrims.

Beyond Place or Time

If you live in the United States, the word *pilgrim* conjures up images of tall hats, buckle shoes, and turkeys. If you live anywhere else in the world, unless you are familiar with our American Thanksgiving, you have a broader idea of a pilgrim that reaches back centuries before the Puritans ever touched American soil. *Webster's Dictionary* defines *pilgrim* in this older, broader sense as "one who journeys in foreign lands; one who travels to a shrine or a holy place as an act of devotion."[1] The word itself comes from the Latin *peregrinus,* which means "foreigner." Pilgrims were travelers and were, therefore, foreigners because they had left their own homes to journey to other lands seeking a holy place.

Church history is filled with accounts of people who made pilgrimages to places that were considered sacred because of their association with Christ or with a miracle said to have occurred there. The travelers usually sought a specific experience such as repentance or healing or they simply went to these sacred places out of devotion to Christ. As pilgrims, they traveled with a purpose. Their goal was not to see the sights in the foreign lands they passed through but to reach a place where they expected an encounter with God.

We do not pay homage to shrines today and for good reason—our focus is on the living Christ and not on a physical place. We do visit the places that were significant in the life of Christ or the history of the church and we are inspired by these places, even drawn to worship God more fully because of them, but we don't depend on them to prove our devotion before God.

Our work among Muslims has shown us a vivid contrast to the Christian's freedom from focus on a place. Every Muslim who desires to be faithful has the prophet's declared holy site, Mecca, on his heart. It influences the way he prays and it influences his eternity. A Muslim must pray five times a day, always toward the east facing Mecca, and he must make a pilgrimage to Mecca in his lifetime. Without these two religious acts, even the most devoted Muslim can never hope to please God and enter paradise. The pilgrimage poses no problem for a wealthy merchant who has money to pay for a flight to Saudi Arabia, but it is only a dream for a farmer from sub-Saharan Africa who barely has enough each year to provide for his family. And yet the farmer is burdened with the same requirement as the merchant, a requirement that he is incapable of fulfilling. So he spends his life knowing that no matter how faithful he is in the other areas of devotion, praying five times a day, giving alms to the poor, fasting and reciting the Muslim creed, he is lost for eternity because of a journey that is impossible for him to make in time.

I will never forget the faces of some boys who surrounded me one morning as I stood by our car in a Chadian village. We had stopped for a rest in the cross-country journey from our town to the capital city. The sight of a foreigner for ten minutes provides more entertainment than these children have in a week, and so we always attract a small crowd when we step out of the car. Among the children surrounding me were a few *muhajjarin,* the boys who attend local Koranic schools and are required to beg in the streets to earn their living. After the usual initial surprise and delight that I could actually speak their language, these boys asked me how many times a day I prayed. "More than five," I said. "I like to talk to God all day wherever I am." Their eyes grew wide. "And do you pray toward the east?" they asked. Their eyes never left my face as I explained to them that God is everywhere and not just in one place, so we can pray to Him at any time and in any direction and this was made possible through Jesus the Messiah. After a few more minutes of conversation, it was time to continue our journey and so we moved on, but their wide eyes and intent gazes will always remain with me. They had heard for the first time that the God they were being taught to worship was unbound by place or time.

Away from Home

As Christians we know that God is not bound by place or time. We know that God's approval doesn't depend on pilgrimages to holy places. But even though pilgrimages aren't essential to our faith, it still remains for us a biblical truth that part of our identity as Christians in the world is that of pilgrims. How so? The dictionary provided insight into one characteristic of a pilgrim, that of a traveler to sacred shrines, but we look to God's Word to give a definition that we are to live by.

The biblical definition of a pilgrim, taken from the Greek adjective *parepidemos,* is "a sojourner in a strange place, away from one's own people." To sojourn is to stay temporarily in a place other than your true home. The emphasis is on the temporary. It may be a brief visit. It may be a longer stay of months or even years, but the sojourner never means to take up permanent residence. In his mind he knows that where he is currently living is not his true home.

Older translations of the Bible such as the *American Standard Version* actually use the word "sojourner" to translate *parepidemos* while more modern versions have chosen to use the word "alien." For our media-influenced minds, "sojourner" may need to be brought back into the translation. "Alien" tends to conjure up images of *E.T., Star Wars,* and men in black suits checking our true identity. Try telling a *Star Trek* fan that you consider yourself an alien. "Really?" he says, and you can just see the gleam in his eyes as his hand moves to request beaming you up. "Alien" may not really be the best term to use today. But whether the chosen translation is "sojourner" or "alien," it carries the intended meaning of "foreign," of being away from your true home and of identification as a stranger where you currently live.

Abraham used the term in reference to his status in Canaan. "I am a stranger and a sojourner with you," he declared to the Hittites who had allowed him to dwell among them after he had left his own country (Gen. 23:4 ASV). David did not live in a foreign land like his ancestors, but he used the term to refer to his status before God, moving it toward a spiritual sense. "For I am a stranger with thee," he wrote, "A sojourner, as all my fathers were" (Ps. 39:12 ASV). The psalmist further spiritualized *parepidemos* by declaring himself "a sojourner in the earth" (119:19 ASV). Both David and the writer of Psalm 119 expanded the meaning of pilgrim beyond a specific place. It became their identity before God and in the world.

In the New Testament, the writer of Hebrews uses this word to identify Old Testament men and women of faith. (The main texts that follow are from the *New International Version,* but I have added in brackets the *American Standard Version* translation):

> By faith, Abraham, when called to go to a place he would later receive as his inheritance, obeyed and went, even though he did not know where he was going. By faith he made his home in the promised land [he became a sojourner] like a stranger in a foreign country. . . . All these people were still living by faith when they died. They did not receive the things promised; they only saw them and welcomed them from a distance. And they admitted that they were aliens and strangers [strangers and pilgrims] on earth.
>
> —Hebrews 11:8–9, 13

God's Word does not leave this mark of identification to the Old Testament saints alone. It is also applied to Christians in the early church and so comes closer to home for us. The apostle Peter addresses his first

letter "To God's elect, strangers in the world [to the elect who are sojourners of the Dispersion]" (1 Peter 1:1). As Jewish and Gentile believers scattered throughout what used to be called Asia Minor, many of the
Christians who received this letter were genuinely foreigners where they
lived, but Peter uses the term in a spiritual sense rather than a physical
one. He identifies them as strangers, not in a particular region, but in
the world itself. He encourages them several paragraphs later "as aliens
and strangers [as sojourners and pilgrims] in the world" (2:11) to live
their lives in such a way that when others see them, God will be glorified
(see v. 12).

Another letter known as the *Epistle to Diognetus,* dated in the second
or third century, contains this observation of the early Christians: "They
live in their own countries, but as travelers. They share everything as
citizens, they suffer everything as foreigners. Every foreign land is their
own country, their own country is a foreign land. They pass their life
here on earth, but as citizens of heaven. They obey the laws of the land,
but they out-do the laws in their own lives."[2]

They pass their life here on earth, but as citizens of heaven. This is the
essence of a pilgrim identity. We live in the world while knowing that we
do not fully belong here. Our citizenship is elsewhere, and that means
that we can never fully call this world our home. It also means that while
we live in the world, we will always in some ways be different from those
around us.

Louis and I have come to understand this more after twelve years of
ministry in a foreign country. We have a great love for the country of our
calling and feel comfortable there. Our African friends even joke about
our becoming Chadian because we know their language and culture so
well. But they are only joking. Why? Because they know that even though
we live in Chad, our citizenship is elsewhere. They don't have to look at
our passports to figure this out, either. There are enough differences to
make it obvious that we aren't Chadian. Our appearance is different. Light
skin will always stand out among dark Africans even when clothed in

local dress. Our thinking is different as well. Following cultural dos and don'ts helps us to relate well to our Chadian friends and colleagues, but it does not completely erase a Western mind-set. No matter how many years we live in Chad and no matter how well we adapt to a Chadian lifestyle for the purpose of ministry, we will always be strangers in a foreign land.

We are immersed in life and ministry in Chad but we know and the people we live among know that we are not Chadian. Our appearance and our mind-set are different. Our citizenship is elsewhere. Our true home is across the ocean.

"They are not of the world any more than I am of the world," Jesus prayed in the hours before His arrest (John 17:14), but He did not pray just for the disciples in the room with Him on that Passover night. "My prayer is not for them alone," He continued, "I pray also for those who will believe in me through their message" (v. 20). We who have believed in Christ have changed our passport identification from the kingdom of the world to the kingdom of heaven, "giving thanks to the Father, who has qualified you to share in the inheritance of the saints in the kingdom of light. For he has rescued us from the dominion of darkness and brought us into the kingdom of the Son he loves, in whom we have redemption, the forgiveness of sin" (Col. 1:12–14).

Have you given your life to Christ? Then although you live in this world, you do not belong to it. Through Christ you now have a new citizenship. You have joined the long list of saints who lived on earth knowing they belonged to "a better country—a heavenly one" (Heb. 11:16).

"But our citizenship is in heaven," Paul reminded the church at Philippi, "and we eagerly await a Savior from there" (Phil. 3:20).

In the World but Not of It

How should this pilgrim identity affect our daily lives? It's one thing to agree that we are to be in the world but not of it and yet another thing to live as if this is really true. We are to be noticeably different from the world around us, but how?

One way that we show our pilgrim identity in the world is through a different attitude toward the things we own. We know that we can't take them with us where we are ultimately going so we keep material possessions in their proper place, as things we own and enjoy but don't need in order to be happy. We collect possessions as we travel through life, things for our home, for our careers, for our use and pleasure, but we know that they are only possessions and nothing more, so they have no hold on us. We should be free from the drive to possess, and therefore free simply to enjoy what we have.

Corrie ten Boom once wrote, "I have held many things in my hands, and I have lost them all; but whatever I have placed in God's hands, that I still possess." Many people have held tightly to their possessions only to lose them or to find that the material possession so greatly desired and finally purchased didn't provide the fulfillment or satisfaction or lasting pleasure that was expected from it. As Christians with a right perspective on this world, we know that all we have is ours only for a moment in time, so we hold our possessions lightly.

As pilgrims, we have different standards of worth because we view the value of a person from a biblical perspective and not from that of the world. The world places great value on three things: beauty (and increasingly youthful beauty), intellect, and power. Put these together in any combination and you have the world's image of success, all based on what is seen on the surface. Even if we know that these things do not count in the long run, we can't escape their influence when we see their messages daily through every avenue of the media. Magazines, books, movies, radio, and television all remind us daily of what the world values and how we can achieve it, and, in the process, firing a collective national drive to be thin enough, smart enough, athletic enough, good-looking enough, and successful enough to measure up to these standards.

Scripture tells us that God has a different view of us. His view is of what lies in the heart. "The Lᴏʀᴅ does not look at the things man looks at. Man looks at the outward appearance, but the Lᴏʀᴅ looks at the heart" (1 Sam. 16:7). I agree with the statement that "a thing of beauty is a joy to behold," but a woman gifted with beauty is not to let that be her measure of worth. A beautiful face will age but a beautiful spirit will last for eternity.

> Your beauty should not come from outward adornment, such as braided hair and the wearing of gold jewelry and fine clothes. Instead, it should be that of your inner self, the *unfading* beauty of a gentle and quiet spirit, which is of great worth in God's sight.
> —1 Peter 3:3–4 (emphasis mine)

It is a blessing to be gifted with wisdom and strength but they are also not to be the measure of our worth, either in our own eyes or in the eyes of others. The wise man, God says, is not to boast in his wisdom, neither is the strong man to boast in his strength. The successful man who has become wealthy is not to boast in his riches. If he boasts in anything, says the Lord, it is to be in the fact "that he understands and knows me, that I am the Lᴏʀᴅ, who exercises kindness, justice and righteousness on earth, for in these I delight" (Jer. 9:23–24).

The world values what we can show and what we can produce. God values us for who we are. We are His creation, fully loved and sought by Him for love in return. William Temple, in his book *Christianity and Social Order,* wrote, "Our true value is not what we are worth in ourselves but what we are worth to God, and that worth is bestowed upon us by the utterly gratuitous love of God."[3] So although we have personal standards for business, education, success, weight loss, self-improvement, and so on, we pursue them from a biblical mind-set, knowing that in everything we do "we are not trying to please men but God, who tests our hearts" (1 Thess. 2:4).

We have a different attitude toward what we own and a different standard of worth. We also have a different goal from the world around us, one that we will pursue in depth in another chapter, but suffice it to say here that our goal in life is to be God-oriented rather than self-oriented. William Temple also noted that although each of us takes our place in the center of our own world, we are not the center of the world itself. Now that is worth remembering. We are not, but God is. Knowing who is the true center of the world shapes our ultimate goal as we live in the world. "Not to us, O LORD, not to us but to your name be the glory" (Ps. 115:1) is the heart cry of the pilgrim.

As aliens and strangers, we live in the world with an identity and a mind-set shaped by the knowledge that our true home is in heaven. As sojourners we know that we are not here forever, that we are just passing through on our way to "a better country." As pilgrims our goal for the journey of faith is not a personal pleasure tour but an encounter with God and a desire for His glory.

"Blessed are those whose strength is in you, who have set their hearts on pilgrimage," the psalmist writes in Psalm 84:5. The *American Standard Version* translates it this way, "Blessed is the man whose strength is in thee; In whose heart are the highways to Zion." Do you sense the freedom and joy in this verse? Do you hear the carefree song of those who have set their hearts on pilgrimage? This same carefree song is ours when we set our hearts on Christ and hold lightly the things of earth. This freedom and joy are for you and for me as we travel through life on earth with Him.

As I wrote in the introduction, our life of faith is a journey; it is a walk along a path. The path is a sure one; therefore, we can walk it with confidence no matter what and whom we meet along the way. Let God put within your heart the song of a pilgrim and let Him set your feet now on the highway toward home.

Notes for the Journey

Nothing is more perilous to your own salvation, more unworthy of God, or more hurtful to your ordinary happiness than being content to remain where you are. Our whole life is given us with the object of going boldly on towards the heavenly home. The world slips away like a deceitful shadow, and eternity draws near. Why delay to push forward? While it is time, while your merciful Father lights up your path, make haste and seek his kingdom![4]

—François Fénelon

For Reflection

The entire Bible is given as our guideline for living in the world, but the verses below specifically mention "world" in their guidelines. According to them, what is to be our attitude toward the world?

- Matthew 16:26
- John 15:18–21 (1 John 3:13)
- 1 Corinthians 7:31
- 1 John 2:15–17
- 1 John 4:1–6
- 1 John 5:19–20

We are to live in the light of eternity, but it does not mean that we "are so heavenly minded that we're no earthly good." What does Jeremiah 29:4–7 suggest about our commitment to our temporary earthly home?

According to these verses, how are we to live in the world as Christians? As you read, note any verses that particularly speak to you and plan to return to them for further thought and prayer before the Lord:

- Matthew 5:14–16
- Matthew 6:19–21

- Luke 12:22–34
- John 16:33
- John 17:20–23
- Romans 12:2
- 2 Corinthians 5:16–20
- 1 Timothy 6:6–8
- 1 Peter 2:11–12

Suggestion

If you have never kept a spiritual journal, now may be a good time to begin. Many people keep a diary when they are on a journey to record impressions of their travels, sights they have seen, and details they don't want to forget. It is a way to look back and remember where they have been. If you are not already keeping a spiritual notebook, this is a good time to begin. Here are suggestions for three possible journals:

Keeping a *spiritual journal* is much the same as a travel diary. In the journal you record your "encounters with God" through His Word and through the everyday events of life. Some people use a journal to write out their prayers. Others simply write their thoughts. My journal is a blend of all of these plus a typical diary's recording of daily life.

A *study notebook* focuses more on Bible study rather than personal reflection. This can be divided into sections for various kinds of study, such as a section for theme studies (prayer, friendship, Moses' relationship with God, etc.), for word studies (grace, joy, sacrifice), and for book or passage studies.

A *prayer notebook* records prayer requests as well as answers. I usually have mine divided into sections for family, friends, church, mission, and "divine appointments" (people I have met once and whom God has given me a burden to pray for even though I am not likely to see them again in this life). Sometimes I divide the prayers into days of the week as a reminder to pray regularly.

You do not need much time to love God, to renew the thought of his presence frequently, to lift up your heart to him and worship him in its depths, to offer him all you do and all you suffer. This is the real "kingdom of God within you" (Luke 17:21), which nothing can disturb. . . . When once you have found God, you will realize that you need not seek anything more among men.[1]

—François Fénelon

Three

A Companion for the Path

> The strength and happiness of a man consists in finding out
> the way in which God is going, and going that way too.
> —Henry Ward Beecher

> And what does the LORD require of you?
> To act justly and to love mercy
> and to walk humbly with your God.
> —Micah 6:8

L ouis has traveled the bush roads of Chad for over twelve years. By "bush roads" I mean anything from wide dirt paths that are fairly easy to follow because of the permanent imprint of tire treads to narrow donkey trails winding their way at random through open fields. Louis knows most of the roads well, because for eight of these twelve years he was the only doctor for a region of 175,000 people. As medical director of this region, he was responsible not only for the small district hospital in our town of Adre but also for developing a health care program for the remote villages scattered throughout the region. He would spend days and sometimes weeks at a time traveling throughout the district, supervising clinics he had built and staffed with Chadian nurses he had trained, as well as seeing crowds of patients who came from miles around because they had heard that Doctor Louis was traveling through.

Sometimes a person from a remote village would be too ill to travel to a clinic to see Louis. Then the question would be asked: Could the doctor drive to the village to see the patient? After one such request, Louis finished his work at the clinic in the late afternoon, packed up his medical bag, and set off in the direction of a village he had never visited. At the time there were reports of bandit activity in the area and Louis knew that the bandits especially liked to prey on vehicles traveling at night. But the Chadians had pointed him in the right direction and as-sured him that the village wasn't too far away, so he started out in rea-sonable confidence that he would find the village before dark. After driving around for a good while, though, there was no sign of a village anywhere. Increasing thoughts of bandits and the fact that it was rap-idly growing dark didn't help the growing realization that he was lost.

Just as Louis was thinking that he was not in a good situation, he spot-ted a man and a boy walking alongside their small herd of goats. He stopped the vehicle beside them, mentioned the name of the village, and asked the man if he knew how to get there. "Do I know how to get there?" The man seemed more surprised at Louis's question than at the presence of a for-eigner driving around lost in the middle of the African bush. "How couldn't I know? It's my own village." Louis felt relieved at this encouraging news but decided not to rely on verbal instructions alone and asked if the man would go with him. The man agreed, left his son with instructions for car-ing for the goats, and got in the car. Louis immediately relaxed. He put the car in gear and drove off once more into the bush.

What made the difference for Louis that he could now relax? In real-ity he was no better off than before. His circumstances were the same. It was still getting dark and bandits were still a possibility. He still did not know the way to the village. But there was one significant difference: he was no longer alone, and the one who was with him knew the way.

The same is true for our journey of faith. "God with us" is a message that we hear most often at Christmas when sermons and Christmas cards refer to His advent to earth in the form of His Son, Jesus. But God's pres-ence with us is not just a Christmas message for once a year. It is a real-ity for every day of our lives. God does not just point us in the right direction, give us directions, and then send us on our way. He comes along with us. He gives us not only the light of His Word but also the light of His presence.

I'm Not Going if You're Not with Me!

In one of the most poignant conversations in the Old Testament, Moses asks God for help (Exod. 33:12–17). If ever there was an overwhelmed CEO of a large company, it was Moses. He had the daunting task of bringing the people of Israel out of Egypt and leading them through the desert into a new land of their own. The journey they have undertaken is not at all easy and no one feels the difficulty of their circumstances more than their leader. Moses has given of himself tirelessly to the Israelites and has received little in return but complaints, bitterness, and outright rebellion. In this conversation with God, Moses almost seems to plead desperately for help, and we can understand why after all that he has been through. "You have been telling me, 'Lead these people,'" he cries out, "but you have not let me know whom you will send with me" (v. 12). *This is more than I can handle alone, God . . . send help!*

When Moses comes to God with this plea, he perhaps has a few capable leaders in the camp in mind for the job, but God gives him a far better response than he ever could have hoped for. Rather than merely promising help, God promises Himself. "The LORD replied, 'My Presence will go with you, and I will give you rest'" (v. 14). I can almost see Moses looking up in amazement and relief. Louis's feeling when the Chadian shepherd slid into the front seat beside him must have been minuscule compared to what Moses felt when God said, "I will go with you."

Moses grabbed on to God's promise and went on to declare that unless His Presence went with them they should not even bother to continue the journey, for "How will anyone know that you are pleased with me and with your people unless you go with us? What else will distinguish me and your people from all the other people on the face of the earth?" And God responds wonderfully to Moses' deep desire for His Presence with the assurance, "I will do the very thing you have asked, because I am pleased with you and I know you by name."

Having God's presence with him was not just a desire on the part of Moses and so God graciously agreed to go along with it. It was God's desire and God initiated it. When we read through the Bible, we see that God's desire has always been to accompany us through life. He never means for us to be alone on the path of faith. He always intends to be by our side.

Walking with God

God Himself refers to our life of faith in terms of movement. Unlike the picture I have painted in an earlier chapter, however, of travelers barreling down the road in a land cruiser, the Bible speaks of our journey as a walk.

The earliest reference to walking comes in the Garden of Eden, and it is God who is walking in the cool of the day. He walks through the garden looking for Adam and Eve to join Him. From the very beginning, it is God who takes the initiative toward us. He seeks our company and desires us to walk in the way He is going.

Throughout the Old Testament we see references to walking. Later in Genesis, God appears to one man, Abraham, and says to him, "I am God Almighty; walk before me and be blameless" (Gen. 17:1). In Deuteronomy, the command to walk extends to all of God's people as He commands the nation of Israel to "walk in all the way that the LORD your God has commanded you" (5:33). This command to walk comes with a promise: "so that you may live and prosper and prolong your days in the land that you will possess" (v. 33).

The psalms are filled with references to walking in God's truth. David and other writers of the psalms count as blessed the people "who walk in the light of your presence, O LORD" (89:15). The Old Testament prophets cry out against the people of Israel who have lost sight of God's presence in their lives and so have lost His blessing. Instead of walking in the light, Isaiah mourns, they "walk in deep shadows" (Isa. 59:9) and "stumble as if it were twilight" (v. 10).

In the New Testament, God sends His Son into a world long darkened by sin, and in Christ we find the light we need to walk by. "I am the light of the world," Jesus says. "Whoever follows me will never walk in darkness, but will have the light of life" (John 8:12). The book of Acts and New Testament letters were written to encourage us as followers of Christ to "walk in the light, as he is in the light" (1 John 1:7).

Finally, in the book of Revelation, in the midst of a stern wake-up call to the church at Sardis, there is a poignant return to that first walk in the garden and to what God has desired all along from His people. In a church that has an external appearance of life but is internally dead, God finds a few people among them "who have not soiled their clothes" (Rev. 3:4). But these few, He says, "will walk with me, dressed in white, for they are worthy" (v. 4).

From Genesis to Revelation, we see that God is looking for a people to walk with Him.

A Walk That Never Took Place

I have mentioned that the earliest scriptural reference to walking comes in the Garden of Eden and it is God who is walking. He is looking for Adam and even calls out to him; but Adam and Eve have hidden themselves from His sight. They are afraid to face Him because of their disobedience. In place of an intimate walk of companionship and ease, there is now fear and shame and distance.

Their disobedience is serious, and they know it. They have failed miserably. They have disobeyed the one rule that God has set for them in the garden and have not believed that His reason for the rule is truly their ultimate good. They have doubted God's love for them and doubted His Word. They have listened to the deceitful words of His enemy instead.

Neither Adam nor Eve realizes the full extent of their disobedience.

They do not know that its consequences will reach beyond themselves to the newly created world they are responsible for and that the earth underneath their feet will be cursed because of them. They do not know that the sin they have just unleashed will affect not only their relationship with God but generation after generation to come, and not only a relationship with God but with each other as well. They only know at this time that they are naked and this knowledge makes them afraid of God and ashamed to be found by Him.

God knows, of course, the full extent of what has happened. Considering the magnitude of their disobedience, we can appreciate that He deals with Adam and Eve very graciously. When Adam finally responds to God's searching call and owns up to what they have done (after an initial blame game), God disciplines them but doesn't destroy them. In a tender demonstration of love and grace, He clothes Adam and Eve with garments of skin that He Himself has made. Even so, something vital has been broken between them. The fear and shame are dealt with, but the distance remains.

God never intended to set the world in motion and then leave it alone. After their expulsion from the garden, Adam and Eve continue to relate to God, as do their sons, Cain and Abel. They believe in Him and they acknowledge His presence; but they never recover the closeness with God that they had enjoyed in the beginning.

Ever since Adam and Eve were sent from the garden, it seems that God sought someone who would not merely believe in Him but who would walk with Him. He finally found this person generations later.

Enoch Walked with God

The first specific reference to walking *with* God is found tucked away in Genesis 5 in a genealogy that extends from Adam to Noah and his sons. What is most significant about this genealogy is that there is a sad lack of anything to note except the longevity of life. From Adam on, everyone in the record lived a great span of years, but did little more than that. They lived their lives, they produced children, and then they died. Nothing distinguished one life remarkably from another. Nothing, that is, until we come to the account of a man named Enoch. Here we read something different:

> When Enoch had lived 65 years, he became the father of Methuselah. And after he became the father of Methuselah, Enoch walked with God 300 years and had other sons and daughters. Altogether, Enoch lived 365 years. Enoch walked with God; then he was no more, because God took him away.
> —Genesis 5:21–24

At first, Enoch seems destined to be no different from his ancestors. But something happened after the birth of his first child, Methuselah. That something changed Enoch's life and distinguished him from everyone around him. Twice in the midst of the usual phrases and numbers, we find the words *Enoch walked with God.* From this brief account of his life, we never know what happened to change Enoch, but we do see the result: a life marked by walking with God.

The whole of Enoch's life is compressed into one paragraph so we know very little about him. But the conclusion of this paragraph makes it clear what Enoch meant to God. While all of the other genealogy records end with the same phrase, "and then he died," in Enoch's record we read the startling words that he "was no more, because God took him away" (v. 24). Enoch walked with God, and this relationship of walking together was so important to God that at the end of Enoch's life God simply took him away without the experience of death. Why would one man's life matter so much to God? It could be that God had been waiting ever since the garden for such a relationship and found it again in this one man among all the others on earth who sought to be with God.

I have heard a story that explains Enoch in a delightful way. A father was talking with his young son about the Sunday School lesson for that morning. "What did your teacher talk about today?" he asked. "She told us about Enoch," was the reply. "Oh? And what do you know now about Enoch?" "Well," the little boy said, "he walked and he talked with God, and he walked and he talked with God, and he walked and he talked some more with God. And then one day God said to him, 'You know, Enoch, we've been walking so much that we're closer to My house now than to yours. Why don't you just come home with Me?'"

What a delightful picture of the relationship that God intends for us to have with Him. They walked and they talked together for many years and it delighted God so much that He and Enoch simply walked all the way home.

The unique wording of Enoch's record also shows what his life meant to those who knew him. Enoch's relationship with God marked him so much that the people around him could not help but notice it. And at the end of his life they were compelled to write of him "here was a man who walked with God." What an epitaph that would be. Could others write the same of us? What will be the distinguishing mark of our lives when all is said and done?

What is noted at the end of our lives, of course, is usually what is noticed in our lives now. In the spiritual classic, *The Christian's Secret of a Happy Life,* Hannah Whitall Smith observes that "the world will not read the Bible, but they will read our lives."[2] Think about your life at this moment. When your family, friends, neighbors, and colleagues look at your life now what do they notice? What *should* people see in us if we are walking with God?

Notice Anything Different?

There were other men and women in the Bible who walked with God. Not all of the biblical accounts use the term "walking with God" but all show that they were people who saw the way God was going and chose to go with Him. This choice distinguished them from the people and cultures around them. It made them, like Enoch, noticeably different.

Noah "was a righteous man, blameless among the people of his time, and he walked with God" (Gen. 6:9). Just as Enoch's life stood apart from his generation, Noah's life was a marked contrast to the people of his time. We have more details of Noah's walk with God. In fact, there are several chapters more, and as we read them, we see that Noah's walk with God caused him to stand out in a dramatic way.

Imagine what the neighbors were thinking when Noah started building a boat in the heat of the desert. Building an ark the size he intended was not going to be a quick and easy job. There were no lumberyards around for ordering the exact amount of precut planks and no local hardware store for a quick trip to buy extra supplies. I doubt there were many neighbors who were willing to lend a hand to Noah's current project. Building a boat was strenuous work that took time, plenty of time for Noah to become the favorite subject of neighborhood jokes. But despite the ridicule and misunderstanding he must have faced and despite the hard work it must have been for him, we read that "Noah did everything just as God commanded him" (v. 22).

Walking with God did not guarantee an easy life for Noah. God had commanded him to do a very difficult thing. Neither did it guarantee a good reputation. I imagine that any one of us would question the sanity of a neighbor who embarked on a similar project. But what it did guarantee was much more valuable to Noah than his reputation or an easy life. Walking with God so closely guaranteed Noah's salvation. The account in Genesis tells us how God's heart was pained at the evil that was rampant in the world He had created—so much so that He determined to wipe humanity from the face of the earth. "But Noah," who walked in God's ways even though everyone around him was doing anything but, "found favor in the eyes of the LORD" (v. 8), and God saved him along with his family from the fate of every other person on the earth.

In another generation, Moses chose to obey God's calling rather than remain where he was. As a result of his choice to walk God's way, Moses left the peaceful, obscure, and secure life of a shepherd to return to Egypt, where he could well have been tried for murder because of his past. As he led the Israelites out of Egypt, he experienced deprivation, ridicule, and more challenges than probably any CEO of a large company has ever known. But Moses walked closely with God throughout it all, and the Scriptures tell us that in the course of his life he became so intimate with God that "the LORD would speak to Moses face to face, as a man speaks with his friend" (Exod. 33:11).

In the book of Numbers, two young Hebrew spies, Joshua and Caleb, held to God's command when it ran counter to popular opinion. They nearly lost their lives for speaking His truth at a moment when no one else wanted to hear it. Joshua went on to experience God's faithfulness as he led the people of Israel forty years later in the massive military campaign to possess the land of Canaan. Caleb goes down in history forever as one honored by God who called him "my servant [who] has a different spirit and follows me wholeheartedly" (Num. 14:24).

Throughout the history of Israel, there were prophets and priests who were not afraid to speak God's truth in a godless society and were equally unafraid to suffer for their convictions. There were kings and governors, queens and widows, who chose to trust God's faithfulness in the face of overwhelming odds against them.

In the Gospels, there were ordinary men and women who recognized God's power and authority in a carpenter's son and walked with Jesus even when others turned away. The church began with people who heard from these first disciples an astounding message of a crucified and risen Christ who is God's path of salvation from the sin that Adam and Eve had unleashed into the world. These men and women, as well as follow-ers of Christ in every generation after them including ours today, risked persecution and death because they chose to walk in God's way even when it marked them as radically different from those around them.

When we walk with God today through a relationship with His Son,

Jesus, we join this rich heritage of men and women who risked everything for the sake of walking in His ways. We make a choice as they did:
to see where God is going and to go with Him. Such a choice marks us as
different from the world we live in because we have openly made a choice
of identification and of intimacy.

A Choice That Sets You Apart

As I write this paragraph, I am sitting in the Student Commons at
Taylor University in Fort Wayne, Indiana, where Louis and I are partici-
pating in a missions emphasis week. I watch students walk through the
room, usually in pairs, with their heads bent toward each other. As I watch
them, I see not only the direction they are going but also who they are
with in this trek across the lobby.

Walking with someone means that we identify with him or her. Con-
sciously or subconsciously we are saying that we don't mind the identification either, because we assume others will see us. And we know that
when others see us, they can tell two things about us. They can tell the
direction we are going and they can see the one we are with.

Think about this analogy and apply it to your own life. Walking with
God means that you identify with God. It means that when others see
the direction your life is headed, they can tell, or should at least be able
to tell, that you are heading in *His* direction. You live by *His* standards of
purity, honesty, and compassion. You have on your heart what is on *God's*
heart for the world He has created.

This may well mean that you stand out because no one else you know
is heading the same way. As you walk with God rather than with the
crowd flowing the opposite way, you may be stared at, wondered at,
laughed at, and misunderstood. You may be challenged and even scorned.
You may well be considered out of step and old-fashioned. But these
things won't matter because of the One you are with. The longer you
walk with God, the less the opinions of the world matter.

Walking with God also means intimacy. Some of the students I see in front of me are engaged in earnest conversation. Some are laughing, others are walking in silence, but all of them are relaxed; as if they belong with each other; as if they are glad to be together. When we walk with God we can have the same intimacy that I see in the students walking through the lobby. We talk with Him; we laugh with Him and cry with Him. We bend our heads in His direction to hear what He has to say, and He bends His ear to us to hear what is on our hearts. Sometimes we walk together in silence. But whether our walk involves earnest conversation, laughter, tears, or silence, we are together, and that is what really matters.

Intimacy with God will also mark you as different from those around you. Leaning toward God and giving Him your ear means you are automatically leaning away from the other voices that surround you. The more you lean away from the world's myriad voices, the less you will hear them clamoring for your attention, insisting that you follow their paths to peace, fulfillment, happiness, and security. "When once you have found God," observed François Fénelon, "you will realize that you need not seek anything more among men."[3] The world will notice. You are no longer interested in what it has to offer because quite simply you have found everything you need in Christ.

But again being different will cease to matter. As you walk with God, you will come to know Him; and as you come to know Him, you will grow to love Him more and more. You will be glad to be with Him even if no one else is walking the same way.

J. I. Packer writes in his book *Knowing God* of a walk that made an impression on him: "I walked in the sunshine with a scholar who had effectively forfeited his prospects of academic advancement by clashing with church dignitaries over the gospel of grace. 'But it doesn't matter,' he said at length, 'for I've known God and they haven't.' The remark," Packer continues, "was a mere parenthesis, a passing comment on something I had said, but it has stuck with me, and set me thinking."[4]

What stuck with J. I. Packer was the way his friend so naturally spoke of knowing God. It may well have been what led Packer to write an entire book on the subject. The incident was used, at least, to begin a chapter titled, "The People Who Know Their God." What challenges me as I read this account is the way the scholar dismissed so casually what he had lost in the eyes of the world. The church dignitaries had apparently walked away from the gospel of grace, but he had chosen to stand by it. They leaned their ears to other voices, but he steadfastly identified with the words of His Lord. Identification with Christ cost this biblical scholar advancement in his career as a theologian. But intimacy with Christ put it all in perspective. "It doesn't matter," he said, "for I've known God."

God walked in the garden in the cool of the day and found no one to walk with Him. Then came Enoch, then Noah, then Moses, Joshua, and Caleb, and afterward other men and women throughout the centuries who have dared to walk with God even when it marked their lives as noticeably different from those around them, even when it cost them something to be identified with Him. Are you willing to do the same?

What will your epitaph be at the end of your sojourn here on earth? As for me, I hope it will be "She walked with God."

Notes for the Journey

Try to take an attitude towards God, not of forced conversation such as you maintain with persons towards whom you stand on ceremony and address in a mere complimentary fashion, but such as you observe towards a dear friend with whom you are under no restraint, and who is under none with you. Such friends meet and talk and listen, or are silent, content to be together saying nothing. They do not weigh what they will say, they insinuate nothing, have no hidden agenda, all comes forth in truth and love regardless of how it is said. We can never be as real with our best earthly friends as fully as we could wish, but we can be so to any extent with God.[5]

—François Fénelon

For Reflection

In your own words, what do these verses say about walking with God?

- Deuteronomy 5:32–33
- Joshua 22:5
- Jeremiah 6:16
- Jeremiah 7:22–23
- 1 John 1:5–7

What does living in God's presence mean for us according to these verses?

- Psalm 16:8–11
- Psalm 32:8
- Psalm 73:23–28
- Psalm 89:15–16
- Isaiah 43:2–7
- Zechariah 8:23

Suggestion

Use Psalm 139 as a springboard for praise and prayer during this week.

We must know before we can love. In order to know God we must often think of him. When we finally love him, we shall automatically think of him all the time, because our heart will be with our treasure....

This one good I will be able to say: Until I die, I should have done everything I could to love him.[1]

—Brother Lawrence

Four

A Focus for the Path

Christ is not valued at all, unless he is valued above all.
>   —Augustine

> My soul yearns, even faints,
>   for the courts of the LORD;
> my heart and my flesh cry out
>   for the living God.
>   —Psalm 84:2

P salm 84 is a psalm that defines pilgrimage. I come to it often for encouragement and the Lord always speaks to me through it. Perhaps this is because I have spent most of my adult life, due to our missionary career, like a wandering nomad with no real home of my own and pitching my tent wherever the Lord directs. Throughout these years of following His path that has led us from our native North Carolina to South Carolina for medical and Bible training, then on to Belgium for French study, and finally to Chad for ministry, the Lord has used Psalm 84 to show me the heart of a pilgrim. As I read it, I want to have this same heart.

How do we do this? How do we live in the world with a pilgrim mentality; that is, admitting that although our lives are bound to earth at the moment, it is only a small moment in the face of eternity and we are really just passing through? And how do we live while we are here in such a way that when others see us, God will be glorified? These are questions that Psalm 84 answers for us. From the beginning we see that the psalmist defines pilgrimage in terms of a single-minded heart.

Psalm 84 opens with words of longing:

> How lovely is your dwelling place,
>   O LORD Almighty!
> My soul yearns, even faints,
>   for the courts of the LORD;
> my heart and my flesh cry out
>   for the living God.
>
> —Psalm 84:1–2

Notice the verbs in these verses. Yearning. Fainting. Crying out. To yearn is to long for something intensely. Fainting and crying out are responses of deep emotion. The psalmist is filled with passion in these opening lines of his song. What is he longing for? His soul yearns for the courts of the Lord. His heart and his flesh cry out for the living God. The psalmist has a passionate longing for God, and that longing focuses his heart and mind in one direction, toward the place where God dwells among His people.

When we say someone has a passion for something, what do we mean? I say I have a passion for quotes. I love the rhythm of words and the clarity of ideas well-expressed, so I collect them like others collect figurines. A good quote can make me stop everything I'm doing and forget anything else I'm hearing until I write it down. Louis has become so used to this habit that when he sees me looking around distractedly, he points to a pen and paper. He knows that my focus is in one direction only until the words I've just heard or read are captured on paper.

On the other hand, I have no passion whatsoever for football. How do I know this? Because when a football game is on television and Louis and our son, Scott, are practically glued to the set with their bodies leaning forward and their eyes riveted to tiny figures of men running around each other on the screen, my mind turns off. When I hear their shouts of exultation or the cries of agony that suggest the end of the world, I am unmoved. During a game, though, little can rival the passion of Louis and Scott for what's happening on that television set.

Passion stirs our hearts. Passion motivates us to action. Passion is strong enough to make us forget ourselves. It keeps our eyes riveted and moves us emotionally, physically, and spiritually toward the object of interest. Passion gives us single-minded focus.

The best example I have seen recently of such directed focus is from my five-year-old nephew, Wesley. He has a passion for his uncle Louis. Wesley doesn't get to see his uncle Louis that often so when we are in the States and are at Wesley's house for a visit, he has eyes for no one else. Just three weeks ago we were visiting Louis's sister, Cantey, and happened to still be at her house when Wesley came home from school. The minute he came through the door and saw his uncle Louis, his face looked surprised and then lit up with a big smile. I can still see him moving from the door toward the group of us sitting at the table, his face beaming with delight, his eyes on Louis the entire way until he reached his uncle and gave him a big hug. Never mind the rest of us in the room. Uncle Louis was there and Wesley saw no one else.

That is focus, and that is what the writer expresses in the opening sentences of Psalm 84: "How lovely is your dwelling place, O LORD" (v. 1). The psalmist's physical eyes are directed toward the temple in Jerusalem, the place that symbolized to the Israelites God's presence among them: "My heart and my flesh cry out for the living God" (v. 2). The psalmist's spiritual eyes, the eyes of his heart, are riveted toward the living God.

I can apply these verbs of longing to my own heart. How passionate am I about the things of God? How much does a desire for Him motivate the direction I move in my life? My eyes ... where are they looking? What am I focused on so that I am always moving toward it with both delight and anticipation? My heart . . . where is it directed? What do I yearn for? What do I cry out for in my innermost being?

Think about your day and ask these questions: When I awake in the morning, where do my thoughts turn? To the myriad details of the day ahead? Or to the Lord?

He is there; His eyes are on you, waiting for you to wake up. Before you speak a word, you can turn the eyes of your heart in His direction and begin the day with Him before even getting out of the bed.

When you walk through your day, are you aware that you are in His presence? Do you talk with Jesus throughout the day and in this way turn your eyes constantly toward Him?

When you lie in bed at night, who is the last one on your mind? Your final moments can be a gaze at Him, speaking words of thanksgiving for the day and for His presence. When you awake in the morning, Christ is already there. You awake in His presence. When you go through the day, driving in the car to the office, to the store, or to school, when you work, shop, sit at the computer, talk on the phone, Christ is with you. When you go to sleep at night He is still there. You sleep in His presence.

"But the eyes of the LORD are on those who fear him, on those whose hope is in his unfailing love" (Ps. 33:18). God turns His gaze constantly toward His people. It is a gaze of loving-kindness and faithfulness. The heart of a pilgrim recognizes this and returns the gaze.

I have found, though, that keeping my heart gaze on Christ is not easy. More often than not I am gazing either at myself or at the world around me. Too much focus on self inevitably brings dissatisfaction with self. By this I mean focusing my attention on my problems, my appearance, my reputation, or on the things around me that I would like to have but don't have. Too long a gaze in the mirror of self makes me dissatisfied with what I see or with what I have. Too much focus on the world can bring on despair. There is not much that I see in the media which inspires hope for a better world.

The solution to this dissatisfaction and despair brought on by a wrong focus is to turn my gaze elsewhere. In my first book *A Quiet Center,* I wrote about learning to rest in God's presence and suggested the phrase "Sit down inside" as an image of resting.[2] Now I want to suggest another image for keeping our heart gaze in the right place: turn away from the mirror.

Turn Away from the Mirror

Several years ago Dave MacMillan, a missionary in Thailand with WEC International, came to Chad to speak during our annual field conference. Dave's ministry of worship and teaching was a great blessing to our mission team and from his messages the Lord put an image in my mind that I have never forgotten. The image is simple, but it has become an effective aid in helping me to keep my focus in the right direction: *Turn away from the mirror.*

What does this image suggest to you? For me the words "Turn away from the mirror" are both a command and a direction. The command is to "about-face" and the direction is away from myself. Turning away from the mirror means to make a deliberate decision to put my back to the mirror of self. Too long a gaze at this mirror is sure to bring problems.

One problem with gazing too long at the mirror of self is what I end up seeing. Not a pretty sight usually if I'm honest! The longer the gaze the more I am aware of the flaws and wrinkles of my life. The more I focus on these negatives, the more dissatisfied and disgruntled I become. A focus on self is a sure way to kill joy in life because I am never satisfied with what I see.

Another problem with gazing too long at the mirror is what I stop seeing. Wrapped up in myself, I no longer see Jesus with me. In fact, the more I gaze in the mirror the farther it puts Jesus behind me. Only when I turn away from the inward gaze do I find myself again looking at Him.

How does turning away from the mirror work practically? When I realize that I am thinking too much of myself, whether the focus of the moment is on appearance or reputation or job performance or a problem, I picture a mirror in my mind. Then I do a mental 180-degree turn and firmly put my back to this mirror. When I turn away from the mirror where I see only myself, I find that I am looking fully in the face of Jesus. My eyes are once more on Him, my focus is where it should be, and I return to what I am doing with Christ-consciousness rather than self-consciousness.

"My heart says of you, 'Seek his face!' Your face, LORD, I will seek" (Ps. 27:8). *Your* face, O Lord, and not my own. This mental image of turning away from the mirror can happen in a second, at just the moment that I'm aware of thinking too much of self. It brings great freedom to me as I go throughout my day, freedom to focus on others without awareness of self, and freedom to focus on Christ as Lord of any situation I encounter.

This is not to say that we never think about issues. We certainly do think about our appearance, we care that our work is well done, and we definitely discuss solutions to problems. But one consequence of looking in the mirror of self is that we grow anxious or discouraged by what we see. When too much focus on an issue causes us to have doubt instead of faith, anxiety instead of peace, discouragement instead of joy, restlessness instead of satisfaction, or simply too much "I" instead of "Christ," then we need to make a conscious choice to turn away from the mirror of self. A good long look at Christ will be enough to put our self-issues into the right perspective.

A Heart Quick to Respond

Another consequence of a focus in one place is that it can dull our response to those around us. My daughter, Susan, loves to read and can immerse herself in a book so deeply that she tunes everything else out. In this way she is very much like her mother! When someone enters the room while she's reading, she doesn't look up. When someone calls her name, she doesn't respond. Her focus is so concentrated on the book that it dulls her response to anyone else in the room. Obviously a concentrated focus on a book is fine, as all avid readers will agree, but when we do the same thing with our mirror of self and God, there is a problem.

Self-absorption dulls our awareness of God's presence; it also dulls our hearing and makes us slow to respond to His voice. We become like the bride in Solomon's Song of Songs. No one who reads the Song of Songs would question that the bride is passionately in love with her fiancé. But there is a time when he calls for her that she is slow to respond.

"Open to me, my sister, my darling, my dove, my flawless one," the bridegroom says through the locked gate (Song 5:2). His words are full of such endearments that you would think the bride would run to the gate the minute he calls. Who among women would not love to be called "flawless"! But she is at the moment more concerned with herself. She replies, "I have taken off my robe—must I put it on again? I have washed my feet—must I soil them again?" For all of her professions of love, she is too preoccupied with herself to answer her beloved's call. When she has second thoughts a few moments later and finally does move to open the door for the bridegroom, she is too late. He is gone.

God speaks to us with the heart of a bridegroom. "As a bridegroom rejoices over his bride, so will your God rejoice over you" (Isa. 62:5). "The LORD your God is with you, he is mighty to save. He will take great delight in you, he will quiet you with his love, he will rejoice over you with singing" (Zeph. 3:17). As a bridegroom would expect a heart response of love from his bride, so God requires a heart response of love from us: "Hear, O Israel: The LORD our God, the LORD is one. Love the LORD your God with all your heart and with all your soul and with all your strength" (Deut. 6:4–5).

I can speak glowingly of love for Christ, but the true measure of my heart for Him is in my response to Him. There is no delay to respond if the One who calls is greatly loved. When Christ asks something of me, will I be so concerned with my own comfort or my own desires that I am unwilling to leave where I am and respond? Am I ready to answer Him at all times? Or will I be caught gazing in the mirror, too focused on self to respond to His voice?

If you are like me, you love Christ deeply and want to be quick to respond to His voice. You want to be faithful to obey. You will hear His voice more easily when your eyes are fixed on Him. You will obey Him more readily when you are not distracted or preoccupied with self. If a too long gaze at self is dimming your hearing or your heart response, if it is causing dissatisfaction and a focus on the wrong things, then it is time to do an about-face. Firmly turn away from the mirror and fix your gaze again solely on Christ. You will then have the heart of a pilgrim, a heart noticeably unaware of self and noticeably set on Christ.

A Heart Set on Christ

Amy Carmichael's writings have continually helped me to keep a single-minded focus on Christ. Her books and letters show that she truly had a "different spirit" than even many Christians of her day in her whole-hearted abandon to His will in her life. As a missionary to Japan and then to India, she knew what it was like to follow Christ on a road that wasn't easy. She had a loving family and friends, but at the age of twenty-six she left Ireland to serve in Japan as a missionary. She knew the heart-breaking pain of separation from loved ones. Her service in Japan was cut short after only one year because of poor health that forced her to return home. She knew the deep pain of disappointment.

The following year Amy went overseas again, this time to India, where she lived for fifty-six years until her death at the age of eighty-four. Her years in India were filled with fruitful ministry as she began a mission that came to be called the Dohnavur Fellowship, which was dedicated to saving children, both boys and girls, from a life of prostitution in the Hindu temples. She knew the difficulties of going against the grain, of obeying Christ in a society that rejected His standards.

At the age of sixty-four, Amy fell in a freak accident, breaking a leg and twisting her spine. She never fully healed, despite much prayer and good medical attention. She lived the rest of her life in physical pain. Her world became a room and a bed. For twenty years she never left the room or the bed. She called it her Room of Peace.

In her book *Candles in the Dark,* a collection of letters Amy wrote to the children of Dohnavur Fellowship to keep in touch with them during these invalid years, one of her letters contained these words of advice. They seem amazing considering her circumstances. She wrote:

> There is no life in this world so joyful. It has pain in it, too, but looking back I can tell you truly, there is far more joy than pain. Do not hesitate. Give yourself wholly to your Lord to be prepared for whatever He has called you to do.[3]

Another note shows the depth of love Amy had for the One she had chosen to follow so many years before:

> You will never regret having thrown all to the winds in order to follow your Master and Lord. Nothing will seem too much to have done or suffered when, in the end, we see Him and the marks of His wounds; nothing will ever seem enough.[4]

Notes for the Journey

> If Christ has our love, he has our all; and Christ never has what he deserves from us, until he has our love. True love withholds nothing from Christ, when it is sincerely set upon him. If we actually love him, he will have our time, and he will have our service, and he will have the use of all our resources, and gifts, and graces; indeed, then he shall have our possessions, freedom, and our very lives, whenever he calls for them.[5]
>
> —Thomas Doolittle

For Reflection

Where do you tend to look for personal satisfaction or contentment or help when needed? Where are your eyes fixed during the day?

What assurance do we have in these verses that God is focused on us?

- Genesis 16:6–14
- 2 Chronicles 16:9
- Job 34:21
- Psalm 32:8
- Psalm 34:15
- Jeremiah 32:19
- Hebrews 4:13

What do these verses say about where we are to look and not to look?

- Psalm 25:15
- Psalm 34:4–5
- Psalm 40:4
- Psalm 105:4
- Psalm 119:37
- Psalm 123:1–2
- Proverbs 23:5
- Isaiah 31:1
- Colossians 3:1–2
- Hebrews 12:1–2

Suggestion

Use the image of a mirror to help you keep focused on Christ. Whenever a temptation comes to mind, see yourself as looking too much at yourself in the mirror and do a mental about-face. Turn away from the mirror and look to the Lord. When negative, critical, or prideful thoughts come to mind, turn away from them. When anxious or depressing thoughts come to mind, turn away from them to the Lord and bring to mind a promise from His Word.

It helps me as I mentally turn from the mirror to pray the ancient simple prayer of the church, "Lord, have mercy on me a sinner."

Lord, loosen in me the hold of visible things;
Help me to walk by faith and not by sight;
I would, through thickest veils and coverings,
See into the chambers of the living light.
Lord, in the land of things that swell and seem,
Help me to walk by the other light supreme,
Which shows thy facts behind man's vaguely hinting dream.[1]

—George MacDonald

Five

A Light for the Path

It contains light to direct you, food to support you, and
comfort to cheer you. It is the traveler's guide, the pilgrim's
staff, the pilot's compass, the soldier's sword, and the
Christian's character.
—Author Unknown

Your word is a lamp to my feet
and a light for my path.
—Psalm 119:105

It takes two full days to travel from our town in the northeast of Chad
to the capital city, N'Djamena. Often when our family makes this
cross-country journey, we stop overnight in the town of Bitkine, where a
small Brethren mission rests at the top of a rocky hill. The mission house
itself is made of rock and is surrounded by other buildings associated
with the mission—a Bible school, a dispensary, and a cluster of thatch
homes. With the absence of full-time missionaries, the main house is
used most often now as a guest house. Bitkine is nearly at the halfway
point across Chad, so it provides a good stopping place for weary travelers. After ten grueling hours on the road, we are very glad to pull our
dusty vehicle to a halt at the top of the hill.

Sometimes we arrive after dark. On one such evening, we had just
arrived and hopped out of the car, thankful that we could finally stretch

our legs, when Louis was asked by one of our Chadian passengers to escort him to the house of relatives in town. As tired as Louis was from the day's driving, with his usual graciousness he returned to the car with the passenger and headed back down the hill. Meanwhile I entered the house and had the luxury of taking a shower.

After the shower I decided to go outside to chat with some of the people who lived around the station. This is when I realized that our flashlight was in the car with Louis. Since there is no electricity in Bitkine, the only available light for the station is a solar panel system. The interior of the house was bathed in the pale glow of this substitute light, but outside was pitch dark. Still, we had stayed at the house many times before and I knew my way around. I shut the screen door of the house, walked across the front porch, and began to descend the stone steps leading to the yard. All was fine until I reached the last step and misjudged its width. My ankle scraped against its jagged edge and I slid to the ground, grabbing my ankle and pressing hard against the sudden stab of pain. That's when I noticed the blood. Not good. So I pulled myself up and hobbled back into the house to do what I could to clean up.

When Louis returned shortly afterward, he found his wife sitting on the couch fighting back tears and clutching her ankle. After examining the cut, which I had been too squeamish to probe closely, he realized why I was in such pain. The sharp uneven edge of the stone step had cut all the way to my Achilles tendon and scraped it slightly. Thankfully, I hadn't managed to sever it altogether! Thankfully, Louis travels with a medical kit so he had what was needed in this out-of-the-way place to suture the wound. It took more than a month of antibiotics and painful limping until the ankle healed.

I learned an important lesson that evening. No matter how much I know my way around, it is never a good idea to walk in the dark without a light.

Just as I assumed that I knew my way around the house but was caught by a misstep in the dark, we can easily assume we know our way around the Christian faith. This is true especially for those of us who have grown up in the church or have been Christians for many years. We've attended enough Sunday School classes and have heard enough sermons over the years to believe we know the Bible well. We may even have learned enough doctrine to believe we have God and our faith figured out. Based on what we already know, we have no need for help in getting around; after all, the Christian life is familiar territory.

Then one day we come up against something unexpected: a serious illness, a broken relationship, a professional crisis, or a national tragedy. Perhaps we need to make a decision that involves moral standards and suddenly we find that we are no longer sure what our standards are. Suddenly, we find that we need more than casual familiarity with the territory. We need more than the pale substitute of our own understanding. We need a stronger light to walk by or else we may slip and very nearly sever a tendon in the process.

Whenever our family travels in Chad, we each pack a flashlight for the journey. None of us want to be caught in the dark without one, as I was that night in Bitkine. Neither does God intend for us to travel our journey of faith without a light. He has given us a light for the journey, the light of His Word to illumine our way. And just as my flashlight was no help to me while it was left in the car, so the Bible is not going to be an effective light for my path unless I am using it. It is meant to be read and studied. It is meant to be used constantly as my light to live by.

A Light That Never Goes Out

But is the Word of God truly an effective light for finding my way in today's world? One has to wonder if the Bible has anything relevant to say in a society that won't bother to listen to anything more than "five minutes ago." How can accounts of God interacting with desert nomads and ancient kingdoms speak to a world dominated by cyberspace? How can the words and lifestyle of Jesus who lived in the simple agrarian culture of Palestine speak to the modern lifestyle of a two-car, two-career family?

C. S. Lewis wrote in his book *The Four Loves*, "All that is not eternal is eternally out of date."[2] We only need a quick glance through our closets and garages to see what is *not* eternal. Think back on the past ten years as well. Sometimes it seems that we live our lives throwing out, replacing, or shoving to the back of the closet things that are out of date. Products go out-of-date and are thrown away. Ideas go out-of-date and are replaced. Fashions go out-of-date and we wouldn't dare be seen wearing them. Computer software bought at the beginning of the year needs to be upgraded before the year is out. The modern world does not have much time for something that isn't useful or advantageous for right now.

Cultures grow out-of-date as well, and it is true that the Bible was written in the context of cultures that now have their place mainly in museums and archeological digs. We take culture into account when we read the Bible, and in fact a study of any biblical passage is greatly enriched by understanding its cultural context. Yet, as important as it is to understand background, the Bible is not a book about culture. It is a book about God and His truth. And what we learn of this truth about God is what will never be out-of-date.

> Long ago I learned from your statutes
>   that you established them to last forever. . . .
> All your words are true;
>   all your righteous laws are eternal.
>   —Psalm 119:152, 160

> I tell you the truth, this generation will certainly not pass away until all these things have happened. Heaven and earth will pass away, but my words will never pass away.
>   —Luke 21:32–33

So when I read the accounts of God working in the lives of Old Testament men and women, I learn eternal principles of how God relates to His people at any time. When I read the Gospel accounts written over two thousand years ago, it doesn't matter that in the Western world no one draws water from a well anymore. How Jesus lived and what He taught are the eternal truths that transcend time and culture. When I move on to the book of Acts and Paul's or John's or Peter's exhortations to the early church, it isn't important that my modern church looks different from the ones in the first century. I learn from them how to live in obedience to a risen Christ in any century.

Through God's Word spoken from a position outside of time, I hear His voice, fresh and personal, speaking to my issues, answering my questions, challenging my actions and attitudes, comforting my sorrows, encouraging my heart today just as much as when the Bible was written thousands of years ago.

A good light is one that has enough power to endure. God's Word is such a light. Because the Bible is empowered by God Himself, it has endured the centuries of changes the world has seen. Other lights of philosophy and political ideologies have shone for their brief moment in history but are now snuffed out. Other books have espoused other words and gained followers, such as Hitler's *Mein Kampf* or Mao Tse Tung's "little red book." But what is their significance today apart from citations in history books?

God's Word endures because it is eternally relevant and never out-of-date. It also endures because it contains truth that has passed the test of time. Because the Bible is *God's* Word, it is truth that God has revealed about Himself and not merely a human interpretation of His truth. Because it is God's *Word*, it is truth that speaks. There are plenty of people who are eager to interpret God and many who have tried. But God has given His own voice to the world and has not asked for our help. We do well to let God speak for Himself.

In the past God spoke to our forefathers through the prophets at many times and in various ways, but in these last days he has spoken to us by his Son, whom he appointed heir of all things, and through whom he made the universe.

—Hebrews 1:1–2

When Jesus said to His disciples, "I am the way and the truth and the life," He revealed Himself as the truth of God incarnate. He didn't say "I know the way to truth" but "I *am* the truth." He was literally truth walking around in skin. Because His very nature was truth, it was impossible for Him to speak anything else. The ones who understood this had their lives changed forever.

"I believe whate'er the Son of God hath told; What the truth hath spoken, that for truth I hold," wrote Thomas Aquinas in the thirteenth century. We would be wise to do the same. What Truth Himself has spoken, that for truth we hold.

The Bible is the only book in the world that offers truth that stretches from the beginning of time through the open doors of eternity. It begins with God Himself speaking the world as we know it into existence and ends with His promise of a new world and of life everlasting to come. It is good to read other books for insight and teaching, but we need to make sure that we are not reading them more than God's own Word to us. No matter how eloquent or entertaining or popular, a thousand books could never substitute for reading the Bible. If we want progress in our journey with God, then we must walk by the light He has given us. As His truth, the Bible is never out-of-date. As a light for our path, it never goes out.

Making God's Word Part of My Life

Because of frequent power cuts in our town of Abeche, we never know when we will suddenly be left in the dark. The same principle applies for flashlights at home as for the road: a flashlight is only useful if it is available. A flashlight in the bedroom is not much help if the lights go out when you are in the kitchen. Try groping around for a flashlight in the dark. This is no fun, especially when you cannot remember where the furniture is. We have learned to be prepared and keep several flashlights at all times in strategic places where we can find them when we need them.

In the journey of faith there is also value in being prepared. If I want the light of God's Word to illumine my path, I need to be prepared to use it or it cannot do its intended work. There are three ways to prepare for effective use of God's Word on your journey of faith: preparing a place so it is readily available for use, preparing your mind to handle it correctly, and preparing your heart to receive its light.

Keep It Handy

The Bible will be read more often when it is readily available. Choose a specific place in your home for meeting with the Lord each day and keep your Bible, a notebook, and a pen as well as any devotional books you are presently reading in that place. Keeping everything ready in one place will help you be faithful to the commitment to meet with God every day. Do the same when you are away from home on vacation or business. Even in a hotel room you can establish a place for quiet time. Space may be limited to sitting on a chair by a window or cross-legged on the bed, but bring out your Bible and place it where it will be waiting for you the next morning, to provide strength and guidance for the coming day.

"Oh, how I love your law! I meditate on it all day long" (Ps. 119:97). Don't limit your study of God's Word to a twenty- or thirty-minute "quiet time" in the morning. Think through your day. Where do you spend your time? When might you be able to read the Bible to keep your heart and mind focused? Where might you be able to take a moment to read? Having a small New Testament with Psalms in your desk drawer at work keeps it readily available for a reminder of God's presence during the day. Fifteen minutes during lunch break or while waiting to see the dentist can bring His promises into a hectic day if you already have a New Testament in your briefcase or pocketbook.

Having a Bible on hand does not mean, of course, that you need to read it all day long as the psalmist suggests, but its availability will mean that you can read it when you want to and it may well spur you on to want to.

Prepared in Mind

"Do your best to present yourself to God as one approved, a workman who does not need to be ashamed and who correctly handles the word of truth" (2 Tim. 2:15). Correctly handling the Word of Truth comes through study, meditation, and memorization. Come to the Bible prepared to engage your mind.

It is important to *study* the Bible in order to understand what it really means to say rather than what we want it to say. Studying an entire book or passage helps us interpret individual verses in their intended context. When Paul writes in 1 Corinthians 8:1 that "knowledge puffs up, but love builds up" he is not making a judgment on anyone who seeks knowledge. In the context of eating food sacrificed to idols, his purpose is to warn mature Christians to not use their newfound freedom in Christ (their knowledge of what really matters to God) in a way that causes less mature Christians to stumble in their faith. Cross-referencing helps us understand the intent of a verse in light of Scripture as a whole. In Romans 10:2, Paul speaks of the Jewish nation as having a zeal for God that is not based on knowledge, so we know that Paul considers knowledge important to our faith. Learning the background culture of a passage adds to our understanding of it. When we have a grasp of the Jewish ceremonial laws, we understand why eating food sacrificed to idols would be a problem for Christians who have come out of these traditions.

The Bible is far from a dull book and Bible study should never be stale. There are a wide variety of ways to approach Bible study to keep it interesting and relevant to what is going on in your life at any given time. Study a biblical character, well known or obscure, and gain insight into how God relates to you and how you are to relate to Him. Read through a book or passage for the overall themes and then break it down into more in-depth verse-by-verse study. Deviate from the usual read-a-chapter-a-day and with the help of a concordance focus on a word or theme such as grace, obedience, healing, or fear. I have had some interesting times in Scripture looking up references to tears, studying the prayers recorded in the Old and New Testaments, and even focusing on events that happened in desert settings. The Bible can be read over and over again and always have something new and fresh to say.

Books are available with practical advice for studying the Bible on your own. Many excellent study guides are also available to help you dig deeply into the Scriptures. A visit to any Christian bookstore or publishing Web site should provide ample resources for correctly handling the Word of Truth through careful study.

Meditation on Scripture goes beyond analytical study to thinking more personally about what you read. Meditation asks questions that bring biblical truth off the page and into your life. It applies "holy imagination" to your reading. David was promised a kingdom but not long after he was anointed as the next king of Israel he ended up living in a cave. That probably jarred his idea of a God in control. What must he have felt about God's promises and power at that time? Mary and Martha asked Jesus to come to them, knowing He could heal their brother, Lazarus, but He didn't come right away. When He finally did arrive, their brother had already died. They had asked something of Jesus, but He had not delivered in the time or the way they had hoped for. What must they have thought about His love for them?

Meditating on Scripture is "not the simple reading of the Word of God, so that it passes through our minds, just as water runs through a pipe,"

George Müller said. "No, we must consider what we read, ponder over it, and apply it to our hearts." Using another analogy, the Bible is not only a light for the path but is nourishment for the soul. Don't swallow it down in one gulp, but chew on a verse or passage to savor its meaning. Let what you read penetrate your mind and heart. Meditation keeps the Bible a fresh and filling daily bread rather than a stale leftover from the past.

Bible study keeps me handling God's truth correctly. Meditation keeps it relevant to my life today. *Memorization* keeps it with me wherever I go. "I have hidden your word in my heart that I might not sin against you," the psalmist writes (Ps. 119:11). Having God's Word on my mind and in my heart keeps me walking faithfully in His ways.

Memorizing Scripture is a challenge but well worth the commitment. I find it easier to memorize verses that are meaningful to my life at the moment. Early in my walk with Christ, I wanted to be better prepared to share my faith, so I memorized verses that clearly presented the gospel. At another time, I needed reminders of what to do with anxiety and anger so I carried Philippians 4:6 and Ephesians 4:26–27 around on index cards until they were imprinted on my mind.

If you are memorizing a fairly long portion of Scripture, it is helpful to break the verse or passage into parts. Work on the first part, a phrase or sentence, until you know it by heart. Only when it is fully memorized do you add the next part. Repeat what you've already memorized while working on the new section. Think of it as a chain made of links. Memorize the first link and then add the second to it. When these two links are memorized and holding together, you add the third, and continue until the entire verse or passage is memorized.

Memorizing verses is like putting a flashlight in every spot in the house. No tripping over the furniture to find them when you need them because they are right in front of you. Set your mind to the task of memorization and soon God's truth will become a readily available light for your path.

Being prepared in mind for reading God's Word helps us to be thinking Christians who correctly handle His truth. We engage our minds in study so that we understand the Bible as it is meant to be understood. But there is also a heart preparation. Light shed on the mind makes the Bible part of our life in the right way, but light shed on the heart makes the Bible part of our life for the right reason. Preparing the heart means coming to the Bible with the right motivation.

Prepared in Heart

We are to be thinking Christians, rightly handling God's truth, but we must be careful not to use Bible study solely as an engagement of the mind. If we do, a subtle danger creeps up on us. This danger isn't usually recognized at first because it actually comes dressed in respectable clothes that often look like this:

- "I am using a study guide and although I'm really enjoying it, I don't have enough time to do an in-depth study, so I'm focusing mainly on finding answers to fill in the blanks. At least I won't be embarrassed when I join the small group this Thursday!"
- "My ministry involves teaching and I want to pass on to others the rich truths of God's Word. I wish I had more time these days for personal devotions, but since I spend a lot of time in the Bible preparing lessons and sermons, it doesn't really matter."
- "I want to grow as a Christian and I know that reading the Bible is important. I do try to read something from it each day because I know I'm supposed to, but to be honest it is mainly just something else I have to find time to do."

Do you recognize the danger in each of these scenarios? The Bible is being read but something is missing. Each person is reading the Bible as a book about God and genuinely wants to learn from it, but God Himself is left out of the picture. The Bible has become a textbook for answers, a resource for sermon preparation, and a quiet time discipline. It has ceased to be a line of communication between the individual and God. There is an engagement of the mind but not of the heart.

During our early years of dating, Louis spent a summer in New Zealand on a scholarship study program. He was on the other side of the world and I waited impatiently to receive each letter that bore his familiar handwriting. When one finally arrived I would take it to the back porch of our house to be alone while I read through the pages filled with accounts of his travels. The letter was for that moment a connection with the young man that I was rapidly growing to love. No skimming the text here. No mere getting the main points so I could report his recent adventures to my family. I wanted to know Louis better so I read carefully and several times over the words that shared with me what was on his heart and mind. There was definitely an engagement of the heart.

The Bible is God's letter to His world. God-breathed, Holy Spirit-inspired, it is His line of communication with us. Through the Bible we come to know Him and through the Bible we hear Him speak. He tells us what is on His heart and mind. He responds to what is on ours. We must be prepared to engage the heart as well as the mind when we read God's Word or we miss His primary purposes for giving it to us: that we might know Him and that through it we might hear Him speak. No matter what immediate reason brings me to the Bible, if a personal communication with God is not my underlying motivation, then reading His Word will be as sterile as reading a textbook.

"Draw near to God and He will draw near to you" is the promise we have in James 4:8 (NASB). God desires intimacy. With Him it is always up close and personal. The Bible is meant to be an up close and personal book even when we study it for a Sunday School lesson. Even when we search it for insights that will be taught to others. Especially then. The danger of forgetting that the Bible is personal is especially strong for anyone involved in ministry. Too many Christian leaders have fallen into sin because in their focus on applying God's Word to others they have ceased to apply it to themselves. In distancing themselves from God's Word they have distanced themselves from God. Nineteenth-century Christian philosopher Søren Kirkegaard counseled that whenever we read God's Word, we must constantly say to ourselves, "It is talking to me, and about me."

Flashlights lose their power from time to time. We know this when the light becomes dim or it fizzles out altogether. When this happens we check to find the reason why. The problem is always with the condition of the bulb or the batteries. No matter how fine the quality of a flashlight, it will not produce light with a burned-out bulb or a dead battery. The same goes for the Bible as a light for our path. The Bible's power to be light in our lives can become dim. It may even fizzle out altogether. If this happens, the problem is not with God's Word but with the condition of our hearts. Examine your heart continually to make sure that it is seeking God. If you are truly seeking Him, then you will want His Word to be a constant part of your life.

Keep a check on your motivation for reading the Bible. Do you come to God's Word that you might know Him better? To hear Him speak His heart and mind into your life? If you do, then His Word will be the light that always shows you the way to Him and the way to walk in the world. Use it correctly and it will keep the way before you clear. Use it constantly and it will keep you from slipping in the dark.

Notes for the Journey

God's way is to take some word in His Book and make it spirit and life. Then, relying on that word, it is possible for us to go from strength to strength. There is always something new in our lives which calls for vital faith, if we are to go on with God, but there is always the word waiting in His Book which will meet us just where we are and carry us further on.[3]

—Amy Carmichael

For Reflection

John Wesley once said, "Let me be *homo unius libri:* 'A man of one book!'"
An unknown source said of the Bible that "it should fill the memory,
rule the heart, and guide the feet." With these in mind, ask yourself the
following questions:

- How do I view the Bible?
- What do I need to do to make it a more personal and effective
  part of my life?

What do these verses say about God's Word? Record the answers in
your journal.

- Psalm 33:4–9
- Psalm 119:89–91, 152, 160
- Isaiah 40:8
- Isaiah 55:11
- Luke 21:32–33
- Colossians 3:16
- 2 Timothy 3:14–17
- James 1:22–25

Read these verses from Psalm 119 and write in your own words how
reading the Bible affects our lives: 9–11, 25–28, 32, 35–37, 92–93, 104–
5, 133, 165.

Suggestion

Before you read the Bible, remember that you are coming into the presence of God. Take time to quiet your mind and heart before Him. Ask
God to speak to you through His Word. Many of the psalms are directed

God-ward and can be read as prayers. Read a psalm before beginning Bible study so that your first focus is on God Himself before the study of His Word.

One way to keep the Bible personal is to pray the Scriptures, that is, let what you are currently reading in the Bible lead you into prayer. This is a slow but rewarding way to interact with God's Word. As you go through a passage or chapter, read only a few verses at a time. Let their truths sink into your heart and mind, then use these verses to pray for yourself and others. Praying the Scriptures assures that you are praying according to God's will, so ask God to give you specific verses to pray for others on a regular basis.

The measure in which I have trusted Jehovah, and acknowledged him, has been the measure of walking in the paths of real life. . . . Paths chosen for us by God all lead onward and upward, even when they seem to us to turn about in inextricable confusion, and to move downward to the valleys of humiliation and suffering. He is the All-Wise, and to him, wisdom is the way by which Love gains his victory.[1]

—G. Campbell Morgan

Six

A Path of Faith

Faith is unutterable trust in God, trust which
never dreams he will not stand by us.
—Oswald Chambers

Now faith is being sure of what we hope for
and certain of what we do not see.
—Hebrews 11:1

O nce when Louis was driving along the bush roads of Chad, he drew
near to a dry riverbed, which we know in Arabic as a *wadi*. As
Louis approached the wadi, he saw an old man sitting on the opposite
bank under the shade of a large, lush mim tree a little distance from the
road. Sitting around the man was a small flock of goats and sheep. Louis
thought what a wonderful picture this was.

In just a few minutes, though, this picture of serenity was shattered,
and Louis was the cause. The goats and sheep, hearing the roaring engine of the land cruiser, shot up from the ground and scattered, hoofs
flying in all directions, to flee from the noise that was coming their way.
Louis felt badly for disturbing such a peaceful scene and looked back as
he passed by. He half expected to see the shepherd in distress himself,
running off to call back his scattered flock or at least shaking his fist at
the cause of all his trouble. Instead what he saw was the old man still
sitting under the tree, undisturbed, watching him go by. Obviously the

shepherd was not bothered by the vehicle roaring past. He had seen it coming and knew what it was. He knew that despite the big noise it was making, it was only a vehicle that was going to pass by and keep going.

Louis thought about this incident as he continued down the road. Bearing in mind that animals are animals and can only understand so much, the flock of sheep and goats could have saved themselves a lot of fear and trembling if they had only looked to their shepherd before reacting. If they had done so, they would have seen his calm in the face of the oncoming noise and known there was nothing to fear. They would also have remained where they were, sitting undisturbed under the tree.

Even though we are human and can reason, we still share something in common with the goats and sheep. We jump, we run, we scatter, at the disturbances that come our way because we forget to do one thing first. We forget to look to our Shepherd for His reaction. Like the old man under the tree, the Lord Jesus Christ, the Shepherd of our souls, sees what is coming our way and He is not disturbed.

"For the eyes of the Lord range throughout the earth to strengthen those whose hearts are fully committed to him" (2 Chron. 16:9). He is always watching out for us. He is always aware of what is coming. He is always at peace.

We can carry this analogy further. The goats and sheep could have looked to their shepherd and seen that he wasn't bothered by the big noise coming but still have decided that they needed to run. They may not have had much faith in the shepherd's assessment of the situation and said to themselves, "This guy doesn't have a clue. No matter what he thinks, that noise is loud, it's coming our way, and we're getting out of here."

It takes a great deal of trust in someone else's word in a situation when every nerve is telling us something else. Yet this is exactly the kind of trust God is asking us to have when we walk through life with Him. He asks us to put complete faith in His Word even when what we see before our eyes urges us to believe otherwise.

A Changed Man

Peter almost made it to this depth of faith in his early years with the Lord. Remember when he stepped out of the boat at Jesus' command and walked toward Him on the water? In Matthew's account of the incident, Peter was doing fine at first. He was on his way toward Jesus on the surface of a lake. But at some point the physical realities of his situation hit him. Maybe it was the chilling wetness lapping at his feet that reminded him of what he was doing. Maybe it was the wind whipping against his body. Suddenly it hit him that people don't walk on water and it was a long way to the bottom of the lake. He stopped looking at the One who had called him to walk and began to sink.

We see a different Peter in the book of Acts. He has been with Jesus for a few more years since that fiasco on the water and has seen and heard a lot in those years. Peter has learned by now that there is a spiritual reality beyond what is seen physically with the eyes or felt emotionally in the heart. People have been healed. The dead have been called back to life. A cross for a criminal has been transformed into the empty tomb of a resurrected Lord. The deep shame of personal failure has been erased by the healing touch of divine forgiveness.

In the book of Acts we see this same Peter who sank into the waves because he remembered that no one walks on water now looking straight at the crippled limbs of a beggar and holding out his hand to help him walk in the name of Jesus (Acts 3:1–10). We see him being flogged for speaking boldly of Christ and actually rejoicing because he had been "counted worthy to suffer disgrace for the Name" when not long before he had lied three times in succession for fear of any association with that Name (5:40–42).

What made the difference in Peter's life? No one can doubt when reading the first chapters of the book of Acts that the enabling power of the Holy Spirit that came upon the disciples at Pentecost had much to do with this new boldness in faith. I think, though, that Peter also came to understand at last what it meant to believe the One who years before had bid him come. He finally realized that the wind and the waves didn't matter when it was Jesus telling him to walk on water.

Putting faith in God's Word in any situation is putting faith in His wisdom. Faith means believing God's assessment of a situation even when "common sense" might tell you otherwise. Faith means a willingness to stay put while trembling to the core of your being, because the Shepherd says there is no need to move even when the big noise is coming.

God has never asked me to walk on water, but I have distinctly felt as if He has asked me to jump off a cliff, figuratively speaking. When Louis and I, with our three children, went to our mission headquarters as missionary candidates in the fall of 1987, we believed God was calling us to serve Him in Africa but we did not know at that time in which country we were to serve. We spent four months with Worldwide Evangelization for Christ (WEC) International in Fort Washington, Pennsylvania, training to become effective missionaries, listening to prayer needs from around the world, and asking the Lord where He would have us serve. During this time, He put Chad, a landlocked country in north central Africa on our hearts. Chad . . . one of the poorest countries in the world and, at the time, a country trying to recover from a decade of famine and war. In my heart I knew without a doubt that God was calling us to Chad, but in my mind was the distinct picture of our family standing on the edge of a cliff. We were looking down into a vast blank unknown, and God was telling us to jump.

We jumped, and He has been catching us ever since.

Louis and I look back over the past twelve years of missionary service and life in Chad and we see how faithful God has been. There have been difficult moments, to say the least. We will not easily forget the noise of mortar fire overhead and bullets hitting the gate at night. We have been to the point of physical exhaustion serving in an incredibly needy society that demands much of anyone who has something to offer it. Louis's training in Family Practice has been stretched to service in all fields of medicine. He has performed a cesarean in the middle of the night by flashlight because the hospital generator broke down at an ill-timed moment. He has sewn up a man's head after the man's wife whacked him so hard with a heavy stick while they were working in the fields that a grapefruit-sized portion of his skull broke off. He has replaced intestines, repaired nerves, and sewn up fistulas, none of which he had been specifically trained to do. We know after all of these experiences that "the one who calls you is faithful and he will do it" (1 Thess. 5:24).

Faith in the Messy

We look back and see God's great faithfulness. The Scriptures encourage us to do so. Looking back to what God has done in our lives in the past strengthens our faith for the present.

But here is a point to be made. It is always easier to look back and see that God is worthy of our faith in Him—after the fact. After He has answered our prayer. After He has shown us the guidance we've been seeking. After He has brought a heartbreaking or troublesome situation to an end. After the big noise has died down and we can look back and see that the shepherd was right after all to have remained where he was.

Stewart Moulds, the sending base leader for WEC International in Britain, calls this type of looking back *retrospective faith.* As retrospective Christians, we fret and doubt, agonize and grumble our way through tough times with the hope that we'll come out on the other end rejoicing because of what God has done. Our faith is indeed strengthened when we look back and see in retrospect how God was at work. But we are not meant to be retrospective Christians only. We are to have, as Stewart Moulds so aptly puts it, "faith in the midst of the messy."

Shadrach, Meschach, and Abednego were three young Israelite men who showed their faith in the messy when they found themselves in a tight political spot. King Nebuchadnezzar had threatened to throw them into a fire unless they would bow down and worship an image of gold he had made. The fire was already blazing somewhere in the recesses of the palace and they may well have been able to feel its heat when the king made his demand. But they responded, "O Nebuchadnezzar, we do not need to defend ourselves before you in this matter. If we are thrown into the blazing furnace, the God we serve is able to save us from it, and he will rescue us from your hand, O king" (Dan. 3:16–17). These words alone expressed a strong faith in a tight moment, but the words that followed showed an even greater faith, one that went beyond a hope of what God would do for them to a declaration of faith in God, period. "But even if he does not," they continued, "we want you to know, O king, that we will not serve your gods or worship the image of gold you have set up" (v. 18).

In *A Quiet Center,* I contrast a "what if " faith with an "even so" faith. The "what if " faith looks for God to do something and wonders "what if it doesn't happen?" What if my prayers aren't answered? What if I step out in faith and it doesn't work? What if God gives me something other than what I want? The "what if " faith wants God to work in its own way and in its own timing.

The "even so" faith says I will trust God no matter how He works in my life. This kind of faith puts its hope in God rather than in an outcome. "If God does not save us from the fire, as we know He can," the three young men said to the furious king who held their lives in his hand, "even so, we will honor Him and not bow to your idol."

How do we develop such a faith? How do we become Christians who trust so fully in God that even when everything around us—what we see, what we hear, what we feel—challenges what He tells us is true, we have peace? How do we walk on water without fear of drowning when we know it's cold and wet and a long way to the bottom of the lake?

I believe the key to such a faith is found in the words of a pioneer missionary to China in the 1800s, James Hudson Taylor. Founder of the China Inland Mission, which is today the Overseas Missionary Fellowship, Hudson Taylor had extraordinary faith, which was evident throughout his life as well as in his writings. Many longed to have the same faith in their own lives. What was his secret? When asked one day point-blank, "How is that you have such great faith?" Taylor responded in these telling words: "I do not have great faith, but I have faith in a great God."

Faith in the midst of the messy, faith that holds up in the heat of a blazing fire, that keeps walking no matter how cold and wet the night, does not come from a formula or method that works us up by degrees to a life of great faith. It comes by knowing the character of the One in whom we put our trust.

Faith in the Mind of God

Amy Carmichael described in her book *Rose from Brier* how Persian carpets were made. Two workers sat on a bench on one side of the warp that hung suspended from a beam above them. The carpet designer stood on the other side. He held the pattern in his hand and directed the workers by calling out across to them, in a kind of chant, exactly what they were to do. Near each worker was a set of variously colored bobbins. The workers chanted back to the designer the instructions they had just heard, cut from the designated bobbin a length of thread, pushed it through the suspended warp, and then knotted it.

Sitting on their side of the carpet, working slowly toward the center of the warp, the two workers saw nothing of the pattern. They had no choice in the final design. They knew nothing of the whys of the designer's choices until the work was completed. Their responsibility was simply to listen and obey. "But when the carpet is finished," Amy Carmichael wrote, "the blending of color with color is seen and how each knotted thread had its part to play in the design."[2]

Just as workers on the back side of the carpet had to believe that the designer standing on the other side knew what he was doing, we must believe from this back side of eternity that God knows what He is doing. Do we believe Him?

It is important to note that I am not asking if we believe *in* God. Believing in God is a different matter altogether. The world in general believes in God, as we know from the many ways people define God throughout the world. Believing in God is easy enough because to believe that He exists doesn't necessarily require much of us. Religious doctrines and acts of piety abound. Even many Christians today have a belief in God without that belief doing more than skimming the surface of their lives. Believing in God is not the issue.

Believing God is the heart of the matter. And it is not so easy. I find out quickly whether or not I believe God when what He says is challenged by what I see around me. Does God know what He's doing? Can I take Him at His Word? Having faith in the mind of God means trusting that He knows the pattern and can, therefore, make right decisions for me, better decisions in fact than I can make for myself. It is trusting in His wisdom.

The Old Testament is full of examples of ordinary people learning to trust in the wisdom of God and learning to take Him at His word. Abraham spent his life learning both of these truths.

He Had to Believe that God Knew What He Was Doing

Abraham was seventy-five years old when God directed him to make a major change in his life. He was to leave his home and everything familiar. He was to take his family to an unknown place and begin a new life among an unknown people. Apart from the age factor, Abraham was a wealthy man and a move like this would mean a lot more than packing a few essentials and heading down the road. He was responsible for a wife and relatives as well as a household of servants, and his obedience to God's command would radically affect them as well. This was no small move for a man of his age and position. He had to trust that God knew what He was doing. Even more so because God had not seen fit to give specifics. All Abraham was told to do was to pack up the tents and head to Canaan. God would show him the specifics when he got there.

At least when our family headed to the mission field, we knew something about where we were going. We might not have seen Chad with our own eyes but we found information, even pictures, and had a general idea of what we were getting into before we set out. This was not true for Abraham. "Leave your country, your people and your father's household and go to the land I will show you," God told him (Gen. 12:1). And he went. One huge caravan of wife, relatives, possessions, servants, and animals all went with him toward the great unknown because God had called him to do so.

He Had to Take God at His Word

God's call to Abraham included a promise. "I will make you into a great nation and I will bless you," God said to Abraham, with the additional promise that he would become such a great nation that "all peoples on earth will be blessed through you" (Gen. 12:2–3). Great idea but with a rather significant fact standing in the way of its fulfillment—Abraham was childless and his wife of many years, Sarah, had never become pregnant.

When God first made this promise, we don't actually know Abraham's response. Maybe he was too flabbergasted by the idea to respond. Maybe he thought to himself the Hebrew equivalent of "yeah, right" and got on with his packing. But by the time God comes to him again (15:1–6), he has obviously put some thought into it. He wastes no time after God's initial greeting to fire a question and point out an obvious fact. "What can You give me, Lord? I'm still childless so all my inheritance is going to go to someone else."

God does not seem to be bothered by obvious facts. He leads Abraham outside and says to him, "Look up at the heavens and count the stars— if indeed you can count them." Abraham looks up and sees a night sky brilliant with stars—stars so numerous that they blend into one another and could never be counted. "Look at those stars, Abraham," God said. "So shall your offspring be." And amazingly Abraham believed Him.

Even after such a dramatic proclamation and Abraham's renewed faith, several more years passed before Abraham's wife, Sarah, became pregnant and they had a son. Abraham was a hundred years old and his wife was ninety.

When we read the biblical account of Abraham's life from our retrospective position we cruise easily from the time of the initial promise to the fulfillment only several chapters later. We see that God is true to His word because we quickly get to the end of the story. We forget that Abraham was actually living these events as an old man with a wife beyond childbearing possibilities. He had the facts of life staring him in the face for a full twenty-five years while God kept saying to him that his wife would bear him a child. During those twenty-five years of waiting, we see Abraham's faith at work, and it is not always what one would call "great faith." He listens to the voice of doubt from others. He jumps ahead of God and tries to make things happen in his own way. He can hardly hide his laughter at one point when God speaks to him yet again of the promise. But even so, through it all he continues to believe God meant what he said.

Abraham's legacy of faith lives on. Paul writes of him, "Without weakening in his faith, he faced the fact that his body was as good as dead—since he was about a hundred years old—and that Sarah's womb was also dead. *Yet he did not waver through unbelief regarding the promise of God, but was strengthened in his faith and gave glory to God, being fully persuaded that God had power to do what he had promised*" (Rom. 4:19–21, emphasis mine).

The writer of Hebrews describes Abraham's faith in these words: "By faith Abraham, even though he was past age—and Sarah herself was barren—was enabled to become a father *because he considered him faithful who had made the promise*" (Heb. 11:11, emphasis mine).

What I appreciate so much about Abraham's faith is that it is realistic. He faces the facts. He has to face them because he lives with the fact of his aged, worn body for twenty-five years while holding on to an incredible promise. But here's the point. "Abram [Abraham] believed the LORD" (Gen. 15:6). Just as real as the physical facts before him every day was the One who made the promise. When we look at Abraham's life, his own faith wasn't really that impressive at times. But it was always—even in its weakest moments—based on what he knew of his great God.

When this same God gives us a promise or calls out instructions to us, do we take Him at His Word? How we handle the twists and turns of our path or even the promises that don't make sense on this side of heaven depends on our view of God. Does He tell the truth? Do we believe Him?

Notes for the Journey

> But how to get faith strengthened? Not by striving after faith, but by resting on the Faithful One.
>
> —James Hudson Taylor

For Reflection

Whether or not we truly take God at His Word is shown by our responses to the circumstances of our lives. We can read God's promises and still feel anxious or have doubts. Growing in faith is a process of growing in our confidence in God Himself. Being honest about our doubts is a part of this growth process.

Read Mark 9:14–24 for encouragement to grow in faith and for an example of a prayer for times of anxiety and doubting.

What do these verses say about God's worthiness of putting our faith in Him?

- Deuteronomy 32:3–4
- Job 12:13
- Job 42:2–3 (Job 38–41 as the context)
- Psalm 9:10

- Isaiah 40:12–31
- 1 Corinthians 1:25–31

How do these verses encourage us to take God at His Word?

- Numbers 23:19
- Psalm 89:34
- Isaiah 45:19
- Romans 4:19–24

When we do not see God working as soon as we would like, what are we to do according to Psalm 27:13–14 and Philippians 4:4–7?

Be still, my heart! These anxious cares
To thee are burdens, thorns and snares;
They cast dishonor on the Lord,
And contradict his gracious word.

Brought safely by his hand thus far,
Why wilt thou now give place to fear?
How canst thou want if he provide,
Or lose thy way with such a guide?

When first before his mercy seat
Thou didst to him thine all commit;
He gave thee warrant from that hour
To trust his wisdom, love, and power.

He who has helped me hitherto
Will help me all my journey through,
And give me daily cause to raise
New Ebenezers to his praise.

Though rough and thorny be the road,
It leads thee on apace, to God;
Then count thy present trials small,
For God will make amends for all.

—John Newton

Seven

A Path of Trust

Spread out your petition before God, and then say, "Thy will be done." The sweetest lesson I have learned in God's school is to let the Lord choose for me.

—Dwight L. Moody

According to your love remember me,
for you are good, O LORD.

—Psalm 25:7

I wish I knew what God is doing!" How often have you heard this comment? How often have you said it? I know I have said it many times and in various tones, depending on whether my question comes from frustration or anguish. It is an oft-spoken cry in the midst of the messy. "What are You doing, Lord?" "Why did You allow this to happen?" "Why aren't You answering my prayer?" When the questions come, we would love to have a look on the other side of the carpet just to have an assurance that what is happening on our side makes sense, or at least is on its way to making sense at some future point.

Abraham had a glimpse of the master plan that God had in mind for him. He simply needed to take God at His word until it actually happened. For many of us, there are times when we never know this side of eternity what God's purposes are. We would be glad to believe Him if we only knew what He had in mind. There are moments when what He allows in our lives makes no sense at all. What do we do in times like these?

Dr. J. L. Williams, pastor and director of New Directions, International
in Burlington, North Carolina, and one my favorite Bible teachers, answers the question this way: when we do not know what the mind of
God is doing, then we must trust the heart of God. Trusting in the heart
of God means believing that not only God's wisdom is at work in our
lives but also His goodness. This kind of faith requires an even deeper
level of trust. We can hold on to God's wisdom even when life is confusing. It is harder to hold on to God's goodness when life is painful.

During our first term in Chad, one of our twin daughters, Susan, became seriously ill. Louis and I didn't recognize at first that anything was
seriously wrong because the symptoms came in stages. We had only recently returned from a family vacation in early December when Susan
began to complain of a sore neck, and so our first thought was that she
was suffering from the discomfort of the long cross-country trip over
rough roads. But the pain did not go away, and over the next few days
she began to show signs of fatigue that went beyond what was normal
for a seven-year-old. One night Susan woke me up to say that her neck
was hurting again. I led her into the kitchen, where I filled a glass from
our filtered supply of water and handed her an aspirin for the pain. Then
I watched my daughter as she tried to grasp the aspirin. Unable to bend
her fingers, the tablet slipped from her small hand and dropped onto
the floor. My heart dropped with it.

Louis had already been watching Susan carefully for several days, with
his mind running through all of the possibilities for her symptoms. He
had even fasted that particular day seeking God's wisdom on how to
treat her. I told him about Susan's hand as I returned to bed, and we
knew now that something was seriously wrong. He gave her a complete
physical the next morning. When he checked her eyes, he saw evidence
of pressure on her brain and realized immediately that she needed help
beyond what was available in Chad. There is not even a CT scanner in
the entire country, so we knew we needed to go home.

Transportation is a major problem in Chad, and we were faced with the daunting task of getting Susan to a medical facility as quickly as possible. Adre is 800 miles and a three-day journey by car to the capital city, N'Djamena. It is only a four-hour drive to Abeche, the nearest town with an airport, but the only flight from Abeche to the other side of the country was once a week on Friday, and this was Saturday afternoon. We could not wait an entire week for a flight to the capital city. Neither did we want to waste three days traveling over land. We had to trust God to go before us and provide another way.

Knowing that we might be away from Adre for a while, we packed up the house as best we could and left town the following morning. Once we reached Abeche, we noticed that Susan's eyes began to look strange. They seemed unable to focus and her pupils were unusually bright. Louis went immediately to the French military base in town to ask if they could help us. We had heard that their usual military plane leaves each Saturday, so it seemed as if we were too late for that flight as well.

Our WEC mission team was praying, though, and one member, Marion, gave us a verse that was to be God's promise throughout the next four days: "Lord, there is no one like you to help the powerless against the mighty" (2 Chron. 14:11).

At the military base, the officer in charge said to Louis that we were "in luck." Their Saturday flight had been canceled due to a problem with the plane. They were actually going to fly on Monday and, yes, we could be on that flight. Our hearts rejoiced, and we knew that God had already gone before us to prepare the way. We were flown to the capital on Monday. By now Susan was unable to sleep well at night, was constantly tired during the day, and was in danger of being dehydrated. It seemed to us that after we had left Adre we were daily watching our daughter deteriorate before our eyes, and we still needed to get out of the country. The next flight out would be on Tuesday evening and it was Christmas week, a notoriously difficult time to find extra seats on a plane. Would the airline be willing to let our entire family of five board the plane on such short notice, or would they insist on Susan and Louis going alone as a doctor with his patient? My mother's heart cried out to the Lord to keep us together as a family and let me stay with Susan all the way.

Yes, we all were accepted on the flight. We later learned that at the last minute, without any knowledge of a medical evacuation, the airline had decided to send a larger plane from Paris to Chad for that day.

At this point Susan was deteriorating so rapidly that Louis considered beginning her on steroids to reduce the pressure on her brain. This decision was difficult to make since, without a correct diagnosis of her problem, he could not be sure whether steroids would help or actually be dangerous. He prayed for guidance, sought the long-distance advice of a neurosurgeon in North Carolina, and made the decision to put her on steroids.

On Tuesday we were in France, but we were not able to get a connecting flight to the United States until the following morning. By now Susan was in a wheelchair. Three long days had passed since we left Adre, and it was hard to wait another night before finally reaching home, family, and a hospital. The airline booked us into a hotel and that night we put Elizabeth and Scott to bed but knew that Susan would need constant care during the night.

Louis and I were exhausted. We looked at Elizabeth and Scott lying asleep in their beds and thanked God for how wonderful they had been during the stress of the past days. We looked at Susan lying in a fitful sleep, so different from the little girl we had known only a week before, and our hearts broke. All of the tension, uncertainty, and grief that had built up during the past days finally caught up with us. We moved into the bathroom so the children couldn't hear and collapsed to the floor in tears. I had already cried at intervals throughout the past three days, but now I heard great, wracking sobs pour out from my husband who had been so strong and calm as a physician, so capable as a husband and father, in getting us to this point. Now he was just a father crying his heart out for the child who seemed to be dying before his eyes.

We held each other for nearly an hour until the tears subsided. Then

we talked about Susan. She could have a brain tumor. She could be showing early signs of multiple sclerosis. She could have something totally
unknown, and we had no idea what might happen to her. We would not
know anything until we reached a hospital where she could finally be
tested. But one thing we decided that night while sitting on the floor of
the hotel bathroom that we did know and would hold on to was the goodness of God. Out of the quiet that settled into our hearts after the storm
of tears, we said to each other that no matter what happened, we would
not stop believing that God is good.

The following morning we waited in the hotel lobby for the wheelchair van to pick us up. Scott and Elizabeth passed the time outside the
hotel doors blowing "smoke" in the unfamiliar winter cold while Susan
lay on a couch inside, her eyes staring straight ahead, her body unable to
move without help, but with a sweetness of spirit that made me want to
cry every time I looked at her.

Time passed and no van appeared. After a half hour of waiting, Louis
checked at the hotel desk to find out why it was late. He returned to where
Susan and I were waiting, with a look of disbelief on his face. The airline, he said, was on strike and no vehicles were being allowed in or out
of the terminal. They would not even receive calls so we could explain
our situation.

We looked at each other in helplessness. But a verse of Scripture came
to mind that another missionary friend had given us as we were leaving
Chad, and we clung to it: "I am still confident of this: I will see the goodness of the LORD in the land of the living" (Ps. 27:13). We prayed, "You
know our situation, Lord." We waited, and a half hour later the hotel clerk,
who had nervously been watching us the entire time, informed us that
the strike had suddenly been called off and the wheelchair van would
arrive soon.

Due to the delay in Paris, we reached New York with only thirty minutes to go through customs, change terminals, and board our flight to
Charlotte, North Carolina. On the day before Christmas Eve, everyone

was in good spirits and helpful, but they all said we would not make it to the connecting terminal. We jumped out of the provided transportation as soon as we pulled up to the connecting terminal and, while I took charge of our luggage, Louis ran to board the plane with Susan in his arms and Scott and Elizabeth flying behind him. With the help of the airline officials, I made it as well, the last to board the plane that had agreed to delay departure until I was on.

When we finally arrived in Charlotte, Susan was nearly blind in her left eye but had already stabilized in other areas due to the steroids. An immediate CT scan relieved our minds of one fear. There was no brain tumor. She spent that night and Christmas Eve day in the hospital but was home with our family for Christmas.

Further tests revealed pressure spots on her brain and led to the final conclusion that Susan had a rare neurological condition called postinfectious encephalomyelitis. What was the only recommended treatment for such a condition? Steroids. So Susan continued to receive the treatment that Louis had begun in Chad and over the next five months she regained her health and vision. Dr. Blair Bryant, a family friend and pediatrician in Charlotte who took special interest in Susan's progress, told us later that he believes it was because Louis had begun the steroid treatment while we were still in Chad that she was kept from going completely blind.

Lord, there is no one like You. God knew what was needed and had prompted Louis at the right time to begin the right treatment. He had moved French military commanders and major airlines to make decisions that enabled us to reach home and family and a diagnosis for Susan.

Our story has a good ending. Susan is now a teenager, and, although, she is left with a slight visual impairment as a reminder of this episode in her life, she is still with us. Louis and I have the joy of saying God is indeed good—we have seen His goodness. I respect greatly the many Christians who hold to God's goodness even when the results are not what they want or are not so easily seen as good—when diseases that ravage the body result in permanent damage or in death; when something happens that makes no sense at all and we never understand "why" this side of heaven.

Even as I write I think of the stunning news we received this past summer that David Hodges, a young missionary father we had known in Chad, had fallen from a scaffolding while painting a friend's house and was now in a coma. We prayed fervently with many others for healing as well as for strength for his wife, Ruth, and for his parents, Carl and Sandy, whom we know and respect. We read every e-mail that arrived, cringing at the early ones that described the seriousness of David's injuries and smiling in relief at the one that finally offered a glimmer of hope. Our prayers were refueled with rejoicing. The very next e-mail told us that David had died.

Through our church's e-mail prayer news, we receive requests for prayer every day. Someone is battling with a serious illness. A man has just been laid off from his job. A car accident has cost a woman the use of her legs. A family member is suffering from depression. The list goes on and on. With some of these requests we rejoice as a prayer team to see how God has worked. Sometimes, however, despite our prayers we do not see God work in the way we had hoped. In these times we have to allow a place for the mystery of His ways in our lives.

Leaving a Place for Mystery

In the early days of the China Inland Mission, a young woman named Freda Houghton longed to serve her Lord in that vast land. But she had to wait ten years before the way opened for her. We can imagine her excitement when she set sail at last with a party of other missionaries on their way to China. Ten long years of waiting were over, and the fulfillment of her life goal was at hand. After a long voyage, Freda finally set foot on Chinese soil and joined her brother, Reverend Frank Houghton, who was already serving with the China Inland Mission. Freda died before the end of her first year of service.

There must have been many questions about God's goodness at the time. Why would God allow someone to wait so long and go so far only to die? Why would He allow this to happen to someone who was so committed to serving Him? Many friends expressed their sympathy to the Houghton family and, in their own efforts to accept the news, must have attempted to solve the mysteries of sovereign will and suggest reasons why God had allowed this to happen. Freda's brother, Frank, wrote of his feelings in response to these well-meaning efforts in a letter to other family members:

> I know there is an element of mystery. But I shrink from the suggestion that our Father has done anything which needs to be explained. What He has done is the best, because He has done it, and I pray that as a family we may not cast about for explanations of the mystery, but exult in the Holy Spirit, and say, "I thank Thee, Father.... Even so, Father." It suggests a lack of confidence in Him if we find it necessary to try to understand all He does. *Will it not bring Him greater joy to tell Him that we need no explanation because we know Him?*[3] (emphasis mine)

These words written in the previous century remind me of an e-mail I have just received from my friend, Susan LaMaire in New York, who courageously endured her husband's long, painful battle with leukemia. I followed her e-mails throughout the past few years and prayed steadfastly with her, as did many others over this long period of time. Many of these e-mails reported moments of hope. But this past year Rick lost the battle and died. Never once have I heard Susan, a young wife and mother and now a young widow, question the grace and goodness of God.

While writing this chapter I wrote to Susan and asked her to share with me what helped her through the years of Rick's illness when she knew he would most likely die. Her response is worth sharing with you in entirety because it is both practical and inspirational for anyone else who might have to walk down a similar path:

> You asked how I was sustained during Rick's illness and death. There are some things that I did, which helped me emotionally, such as writing in my journal. Writing helped me to work through my emotions. It was also very helpful to have chunks of time almost daily for reflection, prayer, crying out to the Lord, reading scripture, and receiving His comfort. I needed to be away from my family for that, and commuting by train for months to New York City gave me that time. In the anonymity of the commuter train, I felt free to commune with the Lord and deal with my emotions. That time was really helpful.
>
> One scripture that helped Rick and me was Philippians 4:6–7. We both learned, through much practice, to bring each concern to the Lord. Not worrying was a CHOICE. Second Corinthians 10:5 speaks of taking every thought captive to the obedience of Christ. For me that meant not allowing my mind to run free down the paths of worry, but stopping and choosing to trust Him. Sometimes I would wake in the night, and I would have to choose to turn off the worry and think of something peaceful (like swinging on a long swing) so I could go back to sleep. We learned to not worry about the future. We would talk to each other about the future, and try to make plans as we could, to make things easier for me in the future, but then we would put that subject back on the shelf and focus on the present.
>
> It all came down to trust. I poured out my heart to the Lord, asking him for healing. But I came to see that God is faithful, that He is going to take care of me and my kids, and that I can trust Him. He doesn't have to answer my prayers just how I want.

I see from my limited perspective, and it doesn't always make sense. God sees from the perspective of eternity, and it makes a lot of sense. My hope is based on His character, His faithfulness, His love. I never doubted His goodness, and I still don't. He doesn't promise a life free of suffering, but He promises to go through it with us and keep us safe (Isa. 43:1–4).

Rick and I were able to wonderfully support each other. Because neither of us was falling into despair, it helped us to stay positive and made the whole journey more joyful. I am so thankful that Rick chose not to worry or despair. He decided that he didn't want to live that way, and that he wanted to be happy every day of his life, and he was. He chose to live each day to the fullest, spending time with the kids, and doing everything he could to get better (like making himself eat well and walk as he was able).

I miss him very much, but I know I will see him again, and that is very comforting. I do not grieve as those who have no hope.

My friend, Susan, knows that God is wise and God is good. She trusts that He knows what He is doing in our lives, and that He is loving as He does it. Sometimes He even lets us know why. At other times, though, and it often seems many other times, He does not let us know the "why" on this side of heaven and so we allow a place for mystery in God's dealings with us—mystery that does not look for an explanation because we know Him. One day we will meet God face-to-face and then can ask Him everything that is on our hearts. In the meantime, we are left with trust.

Notes for the Journey

Sometimes diamonds are done in rough packages, so that their value cannot be seen. When the tabernacle was built in the wilderness there was nothing rich in its outward appearance. The costly things were all within, and its outward covering or rough badger skin gave no hint of the valuable things which it contained.

God may send you, dear friends, some costly packages. Do not worry if they are done up in rough wrappings. You may be sure there are treasures of love, and kindness, and wisdom hiding within. If we take what he sends, and trust him for the goodness in it, even in the dark, we shall learn the meaning of the secrets of providence.[4]

—A. B. Simpson

For Reflection

When you say, "God is good," what do you mean? How do you like to see His goodness at work in your life? How do you react when things happen that aren't good? What is your view of God at these times? God can handle our honesty, so be sure to be fully honest before Him as you think through these questions. Then consider this statement: we are not to judge God's character by our circumstances but rather judge our circumstances by what we know of God's character.

How do these verses assure us of God's love for us and desire for our good?

- Psalm 25:7–10
- Psalm 31:19
- Psalm 86:4–5
- Psalm 119:68

- Psalm 145:7–9
- Isaiah 40:11
- Ephesians 2:4–9
- 1 Peter 1:3–4

Make us Thy mountaineers;
We would not linger on the lower slope,
Fill us afresh with hope, O God of Hope,
That undefeated we may climb up the hill
As seeing Him who is invisible.

Let us die climbing.
When this little while
Lies far behind us, and the last defile
Is all alight, and in that light we see
Our Leader and our Lord, what will it be.[1]

—Amy Carmichael

Eight

A Path of Hope

For a Christian there must be hope based
on a firm foundation.
—Dietrich Bonhoeffer

We have this hope as an anchor for the soul, firm and secure.
—Hebrews 6:19

Hope is a powerful emotion. It drives us forward and keeps us going when things are tough. It carries us through bleak nights when discouragement is knocking hard at the door. It gets us up in the morning because there is the hope of a new and better day. It motivates us to do some pretty extraordinary things.

Sometimes our travels in Chad take us on a road that forces us to cross a river if we want to continue the journey. For my husband, hope is the motivation that enables him to plunge our four-wheel drive land cruiser into a river flowing with water so deep that at times it reaches to the windows. Each time he steps on the gas and directs the car toward where he has decided is the best spot to cross, his hope is to pull out on the other side rather than be swept away by a sudden rush of water, as is sometimes the case for travelers during the rainy season. We know that some cars don't make it across, because after the rains have ceased and the rivers dry up there are always a few carcasses of vehicles embedded halfway into the sandy riverbed. Most often, a car gets stuck in the middle of the river and needs a crowd of strong Chadian men to help pull it out, usually with a hefty fee for their efforts.

For my part, it never bothers me to be in a car that's about to plunge into a flowing riverbed. Louis is known as one of the best bush drivers around, and I have confidence in his ability to drive through water. He's done it enough over a period of twelve years and knows just how to handle the car in this situation. He stops the car by the riverbank, gets out, and walks across the river to find the most solid sand path underfoot. When he has found the best path to take, he returns to us, gets back behind the wheel, guns the engine, and off we go. There are times, I must admit, that I wonder why Louis chose to steer the car in a certain direction. But even if I do not like the particular path he has chosen for crossing the river, I would be foolish to grab the wheel away from him and try to steer the car myself. I also refrain from a wifely temptation to give him instructions. He is the one who has already gone before us to test the ground.

My hope is not placed in the direction of the path he's chosen, but in Louis, who knows it is the best way to get to the other side. And I have never been disappointed. We have always made it across.

We can certainly have situations in our life of faith that look like crossing a swollen river. Situations arise in life that seem impossible or, at best, difficult to manage and we wonder if the direction God is taking us is the right one. If it were at all possible, we would take the steering wheel from God's hands and maneuver our lives until they're heading in the direction we want. Since that isn't possible and we can't always control the situations of life, we resort to giving instructions. We direct God by telling Him what we want to happen. This, of course, is fine since we are instructed in the Bible to ask in order to receive. Only sometimes, even when we have been very specific in asking, God doesn't always do things our way.

Yet the Bible clearly tells us that "hope does not disappoint" (Rom. 5:3–5). What do we do, then, when despite our asking and despite our taking God at His Word when it says we will not be disappointed, things do not go the way we had hoped? We change the focus of our hope from the conditions of the river to the One who can get us across. We relinquish our control of the car and let God be the one in control. We walk in faith by putting our trust in God's wisdom. We walk in trust by believing in His goodness. We walk in hope by putting our trust in His sovereign control of our lives.

Letting God Be God

The stark reality of life is that even with our sincere prayers, sometimes things don't go right. Accidents happen. Loved ones die. Plans do not work out. Disappointments, sometimes great ones, occur. Tragedies happen, even to Christians. Wonderful stories of near misses have come out of the September 11 tragedy, but there were also Christians in the World Trade Center towers and on the planes that crashed. Where do our ideas of a God who controls the universe fit into such a picture?

We generally like the idea of someone in control when it means that person is taking care of us. I must admit that it is very nice to travel internationally, as we regularly do as a missionary family, when my husband is in charge of the travel plans, the tickets, and the details of when we're supposed to be where. Having Louis lead the way makes life much easier for the rest of us, as I find out anew each time I travel on my own!

We like the idea that God is in control when it means we can just breeze along behind Him, enjoying the benefits of His care. And what a God we have who is caring for us:

> Ah, sovereign Lord, you have made the heavens and the earth by your great power and outstretched arm. Nothing is too hard for you.
>
> —Jeremiah 32:17

I know that you can do all things; no plan of yours can be
thwarted.

—Job 42:2

Because Someone with such authority and power is taking care of us,
we can hold confidently to the promise from 1 Peter 5:7, "cast all your
anxiety on him because he cares for you."

Yes, we like having someone in control when it means she or he is
taking care of us. The problem comes when that individual starts telling
us what to do or when the direction we are being led in doesn't match
the direction we would prefer to be heading. Suddenly we have a problem with control. Suddenly we have a problem with God.

There are many verses in Scripture that speak of God's loving, gentle
care for His people. But other verses remind us that God is more to us
than a shepherd watching his flock by night. He is also a King upon His
throne. As our sovereign King, God is above us and beyond us and is not
to be boxed in to certain ways of acting on our behalf. He is not like us.
He is, after all, God.

Who has understood the mind of the Lord,
    or instructed him as his counselor?
Whom did the Lord consult to enlighten him,
    and who taught him the right way?
Who was it that taught him knowledge
    or showed him the path of understanding?
           —Isaiah 40:13–14

"For my thoughts are not your thoughts,
    neither are your ways my ways,"
           declares the Lord.

"As the heavens are higher than the earth,
so are my ways higher than your ways
and my thoughts than your thoughts."
—Isaiah 55:8–9

How great you are, O Sovereign LORD! There is no one like you,
and there is no God but you.
—2 Samuel 7:22

C. H. Spurgeon expressed this unwillingness to let God be our sovereign king in a sermon titled *Divine Sovereignty*.[2] According to Spurgeon, "Men will allow God to be everywhere except upon His throne . . . for God on His throne is not the God they love. They love Him anywhere better than they do when He sits with His scepter in His hand and His crown upon His head. But it is God upon the throne that we love to preach. It is God upon His throne whom we trust." Spurgeon loved to preach God upon His throne because it is only a truly sovereign God whom we can truly trust.

The problem for many of us is that although we readily acknowledge God's sovereignty in the universe, we are not always willing to let Him sit on His rightful throne when it comes to our personal affairs. We're very glad for Him to be involved in our lives, especially in a comforting or friendship fashion, which are true aspects of our loving relationship with Him, but on His throne where He dictates what happens in my life whether I like it or not? No, thank you.

God is indeed a sovereign Lord who rules the universe and along with it our lives. Because our relationship with Him is intimate, the temptation sometimes is to forget that He is Lord and Master and as a result take Him for granted. True, He is a constant companion, as we have seen in a previous chapter, but we are never to forget that we walk with the one true God, majestic and glorious, holy and righteous. We must never become casual or careless in our thoughts toward Him.

Who's on the Throne?

Another problem is that we may acknowledge that God is on His throne, but decide that we want to be there with Him. Sometimes God needs to remind us that we are usurping His position. My good friend, Betsy, was reminded of this in an unusual way. A situation in her family was causing her increasing anxiety because she could not control the outcome. Betsy knew how she wanted things to turn out. Yet no matter how hard she tried to help them along toward that desired outcome, things were not going as she had hoped. She told me that she knew the Lord was asking her to give up control of the situation, but like all good wives and mothers, she liked to do what she could to steer things in the right direction.

Betsy remembers taking a long soak in the bathtub one evening while once again mulling over the problem, when all of a sudden she heard the Lord speak to her.

Betsy, He said, *I want you to resign from the Trinity.* When she told me about this later on, we both laughed at God's sense of humor. But the point was well taken. Betsy knew what the Lord was telling her. She stepped down from trying to be part of the Godhead and let Him be the One fully in control. Betsy relinquished her control to God as well as her anxiety, and in His time and in His way the situation came to a good conclusion.

In many ways, we are all like Betsy at one time or another. We are control experts. Or at least we try to be. We try to control our environment to ensure comfort and success. We try to control our bodies to keep healthy, handsome, and youthful. We try to control our future by getting the best education, job, or salary that we can. Our culture, especially through advertising campaigns, has promoted the false impression that life is never supposed to go wrong if we are doing everything we can to make it right. But reality seems always to be sticking a wedge into our well-oiled gears and causing problems. When our careful plans come grinding to a halt because of some unexpected pebble in the works, faith falters. But oh the depth of growth for those who persevere!

We like to control God as well. We like to tell Him what His sovereign control should look like, how He should order our lives, and how He should act on our behalf. We like to tell Him what a ministry should look like if it is successful and, by the way since we are serving Him, we should have that same kind of successful ministry. We like to tell Him that because He is in charge there should be no suffering, no disappointments, no consequences of a world fallen into sin, no tragedies that affect the lives of Christians who are sincerely living for Him.

We are very good at praising God when things are obviously working out in our lives. The praise falters on our lips when things fall apart. We do not know what to do with a sovereign God who allows tragedy to happen to His people.

We don't know what to do, but God knows what we are to do. We are to let Him be God. We are to relinquish our attempts to be a member of the Godhead and let Him be the one in control. Do you remember the illustration of the carpet weavers? Life is not a series of random events with no purpose. A Master Designer is behind the warp, One who knows what He is doing and where all the threads are leading, calling out His instructions with an ultimate pattern in mind.

I recently read Madeleine L'Engle's book, *Two-Part Invention: The Story of a Marriage.* As she writes, she is watching her husband, actor Hugh Franklin, battle cancer. While she deals with the effects of the disease and its treatments on her beloved husband, she receives the news of the suicide of a talented godson and hears of personal tragedies from others who are close to her. Her words are a poignant reminder of what we are to do with the idea of a sovereign God in the face of tragedy, grief, or disappointment:

> My friend Dana and I talk about how we want to make everything all right for those we love, and cannot. Her mother died of

pancreatic cancer only a few months ago. We say to each other that if we were God we would make everything all right, and then we stop. Look at each other. Because we suddenly see that making everything all right would *not* make everything all right. We would not be human beings. We would then be no more than puppets obeying the strings of the master puppeteer. We agree sadly that it is a good thing that we are not God; we do not have to understand God's ways, or the suffering and broken-ness and pain that sooner or later comes to us all.[3]

But we do have to know in the very depths of our being that the ulti-mate end of the story, no matter how many aeons it takes, is going to be all right.

Having the sure hope that God is in control does not mean that we float through life with beatific smiles on our faces, never feeling pain or sorrow or disappointment, never wishing at some point that we were God so we could do things differently for ourselves or for those we love. It does mean, however, that despite what we feel, in the very depths of our being we also *know* something. We know that, as Madeleine L'Engle puts it, the ultimate end of the story is going to be all right. "Terrible things happen," she writes elsewhere, "and God does not prevent them. But the purpose of a universe created by a loving Maker is to be trusted."[4]

This is our hope. We know that God is on His throne and is in control and is to be trusted. Such a hope is sure. Such a hope shows us how to live. It shows us that we can live without fear no matter what happens in our lives or in the lives of those we love. This hope especially combats a fear of the future. No matter what may happen in our individual lives, we have a Father in heaven who is seriously working for our good. No matter what may happen in the world, God is at work, unfolding His ultimate purpose for humanity. We could easily look at the world as it is now and despair, but we do not. Why not? Because, as evangelist and author Billy Graham says, we've read the last chapter of the Bible. We know the end of the story and it reveals that God is in control. Not only do we know the end of the story, but we also know the One who is writing the book. Knowing the Author personally, we can vouch for His character. We are certain that what He has written is true.

A Hope That Goes Beyond the Grave

Dietrich Bonhoeffer, best known for his book *The Cost of Discipleship*, lived the truth of a sure hope in God during the turbulent years of Hitler's hold on Germany. A true theologian and pastor, Bonhoeffer would have loved nothing more than to live his life teaching and writing the truths of Christ, but he was caught up in events of his country. As a Christian he felt he couldn't ignore them. Because of a firm commitment to living his faith rather than merely believing it, he found himself swimming against a very strong tide and it eventually cost him his life.

When Hitler's Nazism interfered in church affairs, Bonhoeffer and others founded a "Confessing Church," made up of Christians who were not willing to sign an agreement pledging an unquestioning loyalty to Hitler. Later, when Bonhoeffer was forbidden to teach because of his views, he began an underground seminary. Believing strongly that Christian faith must be put into action, Bonhoeffer soon joined efforts to smuggle Jews out of Germany. At the same time he aligned himself with a group of men, some of them officers in the German service, who were conspiring to assassinate Hitler. Various attempts failed and Bonhoeffer was arrested. He was first imprisoned in a Gestapo prison in Berlin in 1943, where he stayed for nearly two years. During these years he wrote letters and poems to his family, fiancée, and friends, encouraging them all to stand firm in their hope in Christ.

Hope in a loving and wise God in control showed Bonhoeffer how to live in a such a difficult time. It also showed him how to die.

On April 3, 1945, three weeks before Hitler committed suicide and only a month before the war in Europe ended, Bonhoeffer and a handful of other prisoners were loaded into a prison van to be taken to an extermination camp. Such a transfer, the prisoners knew, meant a death decree had already been issued in Berlin. On April 8, the group of men reached the small Bavarian village of Schonberg, where they were directed to a schoolhouse set up as a temporary prison. Inside the schoolhouse, some of the prisoners asked Bonhoeffer to lead them in a prayer service. He led the impromptu service, speaking from Isaiah 53 of the One by whose "wounds we are healed." He also offered a meditation on 1 Peter 1:3, "Praise be to the God and Father of our Lord Jesus Christ! In his great mercy he has given us new birth into a living hope through the resurrection of Jesus Christ from the dead."

The door opened. Two men entered and ordered Bonhoeffer to follow them. The other prisoners looked at each other, knowing this could mean only one thing. Bonhoeffer was to be executed. British intelligence officer, Payne Best, who was one of that small group of prisoners, later described the parting. Bonhoeffer took his time saying good-bye to each of the men, then he pulled Payne aside and asked him to give a message to his friend, English Bishop George Bell. Tell him, Bonhoeffer said, "this is the end—for me, the beginning of life."

The next morning Bonhoeffer was hanged along with two other conspirators. The camp doctor who was assigned to witness the execution watched Bonhoeffer kneel and pray before being led to the gallows. He remarked later, "I was most deeply moved by the way this lovable man prayed, so devout and so certain that God heard his prayers. . . . In the almost fifty years that I worked as a doctor, I have hardly ever seen a man die so entirely submissive to the will of God."

Bonhoeffer knew that as Christians we have a hope that goes beyond the events of the world. Our hope in heaven gives us grace and strength to face death because we know that this life is not all there is. We understand that death is not an end but a beginning, and that death itself is not a fearful thing because "precious in the sight of the LORD is the death of his saints" (Ps. 116:15).

For Christians who have lost loved ones, this hope is very dear. It means we will meet our loved ones again. Susan Lamaire's last words in her e-mail concerning her husband, Rick, express this so well: "I miss him very much, but I know I will see him again, and that is very comforting. I do not grieve as those who have no hope." For Christians who are facing death themselves, this hope brings the calm assurance of something wonderful waiting on the other side of the river. For Christians who are seeking to walk faithfully with Christ in the midst of difficulties, there is the hope that their Lord has already gone before and knows the path they need to take to get through the river.

> For our light and momentary troubles are achieving for us an eternal glory that far outweighs them all. So we fix our eyes not on what is seen, but on what is unseen. For what is seen is temporary, but what is unseen is eternal.
>
> —2 Corinthians 4:17–18

> But in your hearts set apart Christ as Lord. Always be prepared to give an answer to everyone who asks you to give the reason for the hope that you have.
>
> —1 Peter 3:15

Dietrich Bonhoeffer set apart Christ as Lord and took the lordship of Christ in his life seriously. He endured with calm assurance the trials of prison and the final trial of death because he had a sure hope of God and a sure hope of heaven.

We walk the same path of hope because we walk with the same Lord. The hope we have is not abstract, not merely an idea. Our hope has life and that life is Christ. Our hope has expression and that expression is the Word of God. It has power—the Holy Spirit. And it has a history to confirm it—God's faithfulness throughout the centuries recorded by those who have hoped in Him and found Him faithful.

There is a God upon His throne who is in control. His eternal viewpoint gives Him the best perspective for guiding our paths. He knows where all of history is heading, and He knows what needs to happen to get it there. He knows where He wants each of us to be, and He knows best what we need to get there. As we have already seen in the previous chapter, because we believe that God knows what He is doing, we trust Him. We trust also that no matter where He leads us, His control of our lives comes from a loving heart. I for one am glad that such a God is in control. And I have an answer for the hope that is in me when anyone asks.

Notes for the Journey

> [God] is in the tomorrows. It is tomorrow that fills men with dread, God is there already. All the tomorrows of our life have to pass Him before they can get to us.[5]
>
> —F. B. Meyer

For Reflection

Habakkuk is a book that each of us can probably relate to at some point in our lives. The prophet looks around him in despair at what he sees and wonders why God isn't doing anything. He brings his confusion and complaints honestly to God, who reminds Habakkuk that no matter what he sees happening around him, God is in control and can be trusted. Read through the three chapters for an overview and then answer these questions:

1. How does God tell Habakkuk to live in a confusing time? (2:4)
2. What does Habakkuk's prayer in the midst of his confusion teach us about living in hope? (3:17–19)

What warnings and encouragement do these verses give about hope?

- Psalm 31:21–24
- Psalm 33:16–22
- Psalm 42:5–11
- Psalm 130:5–7
- Psalm 131:1–3
- Romans 5:1–5

According to these verses, what is the firm foundation of our hope?

- 1 Corinthians 15:3–5, 16–21, 51–58
- Colossians 1:27
- 2 Timothy 1:12
- 2 Timothy 2:11–13
- Titus 1:1–2
- 1 Peter 1:3–4

Suggestion

Use Psalm 146 this week as a psalm of praise and hope.

I praise Thee while my days go on;
I love Thee while my days go on:
Through dark and dearth,
Through fire and frost,
With emptied arms and treasure lost,
I thank Thee while my days go on.
            —Elizabeth Barrett Browning

Nine

A Path of Praise

Let us fill all our pauses with praise!

—Amy Carmichael

He put a new song in my mouth,
a hymn of praise to our God.

—Psalm 40:3

Imagine a Monday evening small group Bible study. The meal is over and everyone is settled in various places around the living room, chatting and waiting for the study to begin. The leader, Rob, has decided that tonight he wants the group to encourage each other, so he looks around the room and decides he'll begin with Sarah. He calls everyone to attention, explains what he wants to do, and says, "Let's tell Sarah all of the things we appreciate about her." To make sure the group gets the idea, he says, "I'll begin." He proceeds to tell how much he appreciates Sarah's gifts of hospitality and how she opens her home to the group every Monday evening. Then he sits back to let the group speak.

Silence. No one says a word.

Finally, just as the silence is on the edge of feeling awkward, someone mentions a service that Sarah once did for her that was really nice. She looks at Sarah and smiles encouragingly. Another pause. A second member mentions that Sarah is always there for her when she needs her. A longer pause, and now Rob is wishing he'd never brought up the idea. When it's obvious that no one else is going to speak, he prays for Sarah and moves quickly on to the study.

We can imagine how Sarah would feel in a situation like this. We sincerely hope it would never happen to someone in real life, and it probably wouldn't. But the truth is that it happens all the time in our relationship with God. I have been in many prayer meetings or group studies that have begun with a time of praise, which is essentially our verbal appreciation for God, and little has been said. One or two in the room may speak up, but then the meeting moves on. It is a sad thing when God listens for the praise of His people and finds silence.

A People of Praise

In an earlier chapter we saw that a characteristic of the pilgrim heart is single-minded focus. Another characteristic of the pilgrim heart described in Psalm 84 is that of praise. The psalm begins with a longing for the temple in Jerusalem. The psalmist yearns to be there because the temple represents the presence of God who is the focus of his heart's passion. Now he looks at the temple itself and notices that birds have built their nests above the altar. He almost seems envious as he writes:

> Even the sparrow has found a home,
>   and the swallow a nest for herself,
>   where she may have her young—
> a place near your altar,
>   O LORD Almighty, my King and my God.
>   —Psalm 84:3

He concludes this observation by exclaiming:

> Blessed are those who dwell in your house;
>   they are ever praising you.
>   —Psalm 84:4

Does the psalmist imagine the birds' constant singing and think of their chorus as praising God? Does he think of the Levitical singers whose assignment for service in the temple is daily worship? Whatever he is imagining, he is envious of those who live near God and declares that they are always praising.

The psalmist knows something. He knows that when we live near to God, we can't help but be a people of praise.

Have you ever thought about why Christians are always singing? From medieval chants to Reformation hymns to modern praise songs, singing has always been part of the church. Compare Christianity to other world religions and one can easily see why. We have so much to sing about! We look at the natural world and praise God's creative power. We acknowledge Christ's redemptive work on the cross and praise His grace. We experience God's provision and praise His faithfulness. We follow His guidance and praise His wisdom. We see His goodness and praise His love. Redemption, grace, peace, hope, and joy are all part of Christianity's unique message and inspire songs of thanksgiving and praise from grateful hearts. Living in God's presence draws praise from within us. We can't help ourselves, because we have come to know Him and what we know of Him deserves praise.

Nearness to God draws praise from within us, but the opposite is also true. In our relationship with God it is rarely a case of "absence makes the heart grow fonder." Have you noticed? I certainly have. Just as a focus away from God dulls our response to Him, distance from God tends to dull praise rather than fuel it.

When my mind is far from God, my worship becomes stale and external. Maybe no one else notices it, because I can enjoy singing a praise song or a hymn no matter what the present state of my heart is simply because I enjoy singing. But I notice the difference, and certainly God does. I may be singing with as much vigor as the people around me, but my praise is on the surface only. It is worship led from the outside sung to Someone I am hardly even thinking about. I have wondered sometimes how God must feel as He looks over a gathering of His people on Sunday morning. He sees into my heart as I follow the service, as I listen to the sermon, and as I sing the hymns. God delights in the praise of His people. Am I adding to His delight? Or am I dulling His pleasure because of what He sees in me?

So often I come to church already distracted from the morning's rush of activity. This was especially true when our children were younger and it was a major ordeal to get everyone leaving the house in good time, much less stepping through the doors of church with any semblance of an attitude that I would care to have noticed. For this reason, I appreciate a church that encourages its members to enter the sanctuary in silence. This gives me a chance both to quiet my heart and mind from the distractions of the morning and to remember why I have come to church—to be in God's presence and to join others in worshiping Him.

Preoccupation with self, frustrations carried over from the morning, unconfessed sin, focus on those around me, critical thoughts . . . the list could go on. They will all pull me away from genuine worship. When my mind is far from God, my heart is also far from Him and praise is slow in coming. But when I'm focused on God and living in His presence, then praise flows out of a heart filled with love and thanksgiving. It is real. It is from the heart. It is for Him.

When Should We Praise?

The psalmist declares that the people who dwell in God's house are blessed because they are *ever* praising Him. Praise is not meant to be once a week only when we gather with other Christians, nor is it to be relegated to special events such as youth meetings or worship evenings. Praise is to be a constant part of our life with God.

When King David made plans for the temple in Jerusalem, part of his instruction was for the Levites whose lives were dedicated to service in the temple. He gathered the Levites together and counted them, then divided their large number into areas of service. Twenty-four thousand were to supervise the building of the temple, 6,000 were to be officials and judges, 4,000 were to serve as gatekeepers, and another 4,000 were to be musicians.

Leave it to David the musician-king to make sure that God's dwelling among men would be filled with praise. The sole responsibility of this final 4,000 was to praise the Lord using musical instruments that the king himself provided. The temple worshipers were instructed "to stand every morning and thank and praise the LORD. They were to do the same in the evening and whenever burnt offerings were presented to the LORD on Sabbaths and at New Moon festivals and at appointed feasts" (1 Chron. 23:30–31). One of the psalms, many of which are songs written for worship, proclaims the joy of this temple service:

> It is good to praise the LORD
> and make music to your name, O Most High,
> to proclaim your love in the morning
> and your faithfulness at night.
> —Psalm 92:1–2

Each morning in the temple there was to be praise and each evening there was to be praise. The people were never to forget from the beginning of the day to its end their God who was with them. They were to acknowledge in the morning His loving control of the day ahead and they were to remember at the day's end the One who had carried them safely through. Praise kept the Israelites as a nation from having a shallow faith, only the form without the substance. It lifted their hearts beyond a building and beyond ritual to a living God.

We are constantly in danger of having a form of faith and forgetting the living God behind it, especially first thing in the morning and the last thing at night. When the alarm goes off and our feet hit the floor and we plod to the kitchen to turn on the coffeemaker or to the bathroom for

the wake-up shower, the details of the day are already rushing in, eager
to fill up the spaces of our minds. God is so far from our minds at this
point that He doesn't even have a chance to be forgotten. At the end of
the day when our heads hit the pillow we are usually too tired to think,
or else the details of the day won't let us go and there is no room in our
overactive minds for thoughts of God.

We have already looked at the importance of turning our gaze from
self to Christ. A habitual turning to Christ makes us more faithful in our
heart response to Him and that includes praise. We do not need to leave
praise to appointed times and places, such as church or a Bible study.
Praise comes from within and is always ready to spring forth. Something good happens during the day and a "Thank You, Lord" leaps spon-
taneously to our lips. We see a beautiful sunset and giving glory to the
One who created it comes without even thinking about it. A day begins
and we automatically turn to God who is the Author of all days. The
evening comes and, because we have been in the habit of talking with
God throughout the day, we turn to Him to end the day as naturally as
we turn off the light.

Louis and I have the habit of praying together as the last thing we do
before going to sleep. We have been praying in this way for over twenty
years, and it is like putting the period at the end of a sentence. Heads on
our pillows and sometimes nearly falling asleep, we thank the Lord for
the ways we have seen His faithfulness during the day. We pray for each
of our children and for anything else that is currently on our hearts.
Afterward, if sleep is long in coming, I am usually still talking things
over with the Lord in my mind.

I'm almost afraid that writing about this practice may give you the
very wrong idea that Louis and I are spiritual giants in this area, or in
any area for that matter. Far from it. There are often times that one of us
is too exhausted or even too troubled to pray and we have to ask the
other to do the praying for us. There are times when our prayer to end
the day is short, very short, because we're not particularly happy with

each other (so much for not letting the sun go down on your anger). And then there are times when we are both so exhausted that neither wants to suggest it. We just want to go to sleep. But when one of us does finally say, "Shall we pray?" and we once again turn to the Lord, we are always glad that we did. Because we began this practice in our first year of marriage and it has now become a habit, a day for us isn't complete without it.

Going to sleep in awareness of God's presence is a form of praise. We honor and acknowledge Him as our final thought of the day, and God, I believe, honors our desire to pray even when the actual prayer trails off into a soft snore.

What we have on our minds at the end of the day often influences the beginning thoughts of the next morning. The more I go to sleep with the Lord on my mind, the more I find that the following morning, before I even get out of bed or say a word to Louis, I am speaking to the Lord in the first minutes of rising. More often than not it is a simple "Thank You, Lord" as I lie there trying to get the energy to push myself out of bed! But my thoughts have turned to Him, and it is a good way to begin the day.

Beginning the day in awareness of God's presence is a form of praise. We honor and acknowledge Him as our first thought of the day.

Bringing Together the Ordinary and the Holy

Only a select portion of the Jewish nation served in the temple. These designated ones were the descendants of Aaron and the tribe of Levi. From these two select groups, only the descendants of Aaron were priests who could offer sacrifices and stand in the gap between the Israelites and a holy God. The selection went further. Only one among the priests, the High Priest, was allowed to actually be in God's presence in the Most Holy Place, and that glorious moment occurred only once a year. The descendants of Levi were set apart among the twelve tribes of Israel to assist the priests. Because they were consecrated to God, they had no land of their own and did no ordinary labor but concentrated solely on the duties of temple supervision, maintenance, and worship.

The four thousand Levites who were assigned to praise and thank God in the temple drew lots and took turns throughout the year so that there was never a day without someone worshiping in the presence of God. Morning and evening their voices lifted up to the Lord as a reminder of His sovereignty and majesty, His love and faithfulness, His wisdom and goodness.

The remainder of the Israelites went about their ordinary lives and depended on the priests and Levites to handle the things of God, even to do their worshiping for them. In the life of Israel, there was a marked separation of the ordinary and the holy.

When Christ gave Himself as the perfect sacrifice for a sinful world, He closed the gap between the ordinary and the holy. Through Christ's redemptive work on the cross, there is no longer a need for go-between priests. The way is open for us all to enter the Most Holy Place and be in the presence of a holy God, not just once a year but every moment of every day of our lives. There is no longer just one tribe of Israel set apart for service. We are all set apart to belong solely to Him. We are all priests in His sight, dedicated to His service.

God is not confined to one building and we know this, so we do not look to a single place where He dwells. With no temple to maintain or supervise and with no burnt offerings to present before God, how do we serve Him then as priests? Scripture tells us that there is still a priestly ministry before God, and that is the ministry of praise:

> But you are a chosen people, a royal priesthood, a holy nation, a people belonging to God, that you may declare the praises of him who called you out of darkness into his wonderful light.
>
> —1 Peter 2:9

Through Jesus, therefore, let us continually offer to God a sacrifice of praise—the fruit of lips that confess his name.

—Hebrews 13:15

Fill All Our Pauses with Praise

The book of Psalms is a collection of prayers and songs of praise. Many of the psalms were written by King David before the temple in Jerusalem was built, but others were written and composed by temple musicians. Even though we mainly read the psalms today for personal or corporate worship, many are recorded with musical terms that direct how they are to be sung. One of these musical terms is *selah,* which occurs seventy-one times in the book of Psalms. The term *selah* marks a pause in the singing. It is connected with the Hebrew word *salal,* which means to lift up, and so, for musical instruments, this would suggest an increase in the volume while there was a pause in the singing.

The use of *selah* shows that worship was not meant to pause along with the words. In fact, the instruments were directed to fill the interludes with more volume so that worship continued even when the voices were silent. Amy Carmichael reflects on this use of *selah* in the psalms and encourages us to never let our own life of praise grow silent. She writes:

Then let us fill all our pauses with praise! Let us give all that lies within us, not to the voices of the enemy, but to pure praise, to pure loving adoration, and to worship from a grateful heart—a heart that is trained to look up.[1]

The psalmist declared that the ones who live in God's house are blessed because they are ever praising God. He saw only one place as God's dwelling, the temple in Jerusalem, and longed to be there because he wanted to be continually in God's presence. Christ has made all of us priests and has ushered us into a continual presence of the Holy, consecrating even the most ordinary, mundane duties and moments of our days by bringing them into the presence of the holy. As priests who live, move, and work in the ordinary of life's kitchens, offices, shops, schools, cars, banks, hospitals, and factories, we are to offer continual sacrifices of praise as we walk throughout our days. Praise in the morning because God is the Author of each new day. Praise in the evening because God has carried us faithfully through. Praise throughout the day because God is with us and wherever He is becomes holy ground.

There is an old praise song that I remember from days of singing around the campfire. The words are a good reminder of this principle of praise:

Love Him in the morning when you see the sun a'rising;
Love Him in the evening 'cause He took you through the day;
And in the in-between times when you feel the pressure growing,
Remember that He loves you and He promises to stay.

The psalmist knew that to be in God's presence meant a response of praise. He also knew that a life of praise brings blessing. As Amy Carmichael writes, praise trains our pilgrim hearts to look up. Whenever I praise God, I am in that moment remembering what really counts in life and who is in control. Praise in moments of crisis drowns out the voice of the Enemy and reminds me that a greater Voice, wise and loving, is sovereign over all. Praise in moments of joy reminds me who has given me the good things that I enjoy. Praise in moments of success reminds me that it is God who has given me gifts and the ability to use them successfully. Finally, when I set my heart on praise, I am reminded that each day from beginning to end is not ultimately about me, but that it is about God and His glory.

Notes for the Journey

If any one would tell you the shortest, surest way to all happiness and all perfection, he must tell you to make it a rule to yourself to thank and praise God for everything that happens to you. For it is certain that whatever seeming calamity happens to you, if you thank and praise God for it, you turn it into a blessing. Could you, therefore, work miracles, you could not do more for yourself than by this thankful spirit; for it heals with a word, and turns all that it touches into happiness.[2]

—William Law

For Reflection

Read through Psalm 103 and list the reasons why God is to be praised. What do these verses suggest about why God is worthy of our praise?

- 1 Chronicles 16:8–12
- 2 Chronicles 5:13
- Nehemiah 9:5–6
- Psalm 22:23–28
- Psalm 33:1–8
- Psalm 57:9–11
- Isaiah 43:20–21
- Daniel 2:20–22

What do these verses say about when and where we should praise God?

- 2 Samuel 22:1–4
- Psalm 22:22 (Heb. 2:12)
- Psalm 63:3–7

- Psalm 71:8
- Isaiah 61:1–3 (v. 3)
- Acts 16:22–25
- Ephesians 5:19–20
- Hebrews 13:15
- James 5:13

Suggestion

Use the verses above to begin your time alone with God in praise.

As we wait before God we should reverently search the Scriptures and listen for the voice of gentle stillness to learn what our heavenly Father expects of us. Then, trusting in his enabling, we should obey to the best of our ability and understanding.[1]

—A. W. Tozer

Ten

A Path of Obedience

It is simply absurd to say you believe, or even want to believe
in Him, if you do not do anything He tells you.
—George MacDonald

To God's elect, strangers in the world ... who have been
chosen ... for obedience to Jesus Christ.
—1 Peter 1:1–2

It seems like only yesterday that I was a student sitting in a huge auditorium seating over seventeen hundred other college students on the
University of Illinois campus. It was December 1976 and I was there to
attend Urbana, the triennial missions conference sponsored by
InterVarsity Christian Fellowship. Somewhere in the crowd was the man
who was to become my husband four years later, but at the moment he
was simply another student in that vast auditorium being challenged as
I was by God's heart for the world.

I remember two messages in particular from that conference. One
was given by well-known speaker and author Elisabeth Elliot. Her
message was on obedience. She captured our attention by her account
of visiting a sheep farm and watching the sheepdog's quick movements
in response to his master's voice. The dog's joy in herding the sheep was
evident, but there were also times when he was commanded to stop in
his tracks and stay put. With his entire body quivering with canine desire

to dart after the sheep, he remained where he was until the master gave the signal to move. "He had no idea of the why," Elisabeth Elliot said. "He simply knew to obey his master's voice."

She also recounted an incident from childhood when her brother was playing the piano in his father's study and was called away by his mother. When he didn't budge from the piano seat, his father looked at him and told him to obey his mother. I can still hear Elisabeth Elliot's voice taking on the whine of a little boy while she mimicked her brother's excuse, "But I want to sing 'Jesus Loves Me.'" With a wise father's ability to cut to the heart of the matter, Mr. Howard told the pouting little boy, "It does no good to sing God's praises while being disobedient."

As a young college student I was like a sponge, absorbing Elisabeth Elliot's challenge to follow a path of obedience in my life with Christ even though I could have been doing something else. Her words were easy enough for me to hear as a sophomore in college when everything was going according to plan and I had no desires that conflicted with whatever I thought God would ask me to do for Him. The challenges came later, when His call to obedience meant sacrifices that I would keenly feel.

Another message that remained with me from the Urbana '76 conference was given by Dr. Helen Roseveare, a missionary physician with WEC International, the mission that Louis and I would later join. Even the title of her talk, "The Cost of Declaring His Glory," was enough to set it apart in my mind. Dr. Roseveare served in the Belgian Congo in the 1960s and was there at the time of the rebellion when the soon to be called Zaire (and now Democratic Republic of Congo) gained its independence from Belgium.

History has shown over and over again that during times of political upheaval foreigners are often associated with hated powers even when they have nothing to do with the politics of a country. So when the rebellion came to the Belgian Congo, despite years of sacrificial service Dr. Roseveare and other missionaries were targeted by the rebel soldiers.

The African Christians with whom she served sought to protect her, but she was eventually arrested and imprisoned with other expatriates. During the time she was captured by rebel soldiers, she suffered the agonizing degradation of rape. At another point, during imprisonment, she was brought before a group of Congolese to be publicly executed until some of the men in the crowd broke down and wept because they recognized her as their beloved doctor. She was returned to prison until she and the others with her were finally set free by government soldiers.

Dr. Roseveare did not spiritualize the missionary life when she spoke of her imprisonment and the humiliation of rape. Neither did she gloss over how God dealt with her pride as a white doctor serving in Africa. She spoke of God humbling her by causing her, the one who had gone with so much to offer Africa, to be the one in need of her African colleagues for both spiritual guidance and physical care. She spoke of an older, wiser African pastor who taught her gently but firmly that she, the missionary, thought too much of herself and needed to deal with the "I" in her life.

Her message was loud and clear to all of the youthful, gung-ho, "ready to conquer the world for Jesus" students gathered in the auditorium. Obedience to God's call will not always be easy. It will cost us something, and it cannot be done while we are getting in the way with our own ideas of how God can use us.

I remember riding back to the dorm after that evening's session in one of the many buses hired to transfer the crowds of students, glad to finally be out of the long line standing in the bitter cold waiting for a bus to arrive. I was sitting by the window, looking out on vaguely defined campus buildings as we slowly rambled by, but not seeing anything because my mind was filled with the message. The Lord had already stirred in my heart a desire to be involved in His world from John Stott's biblical expositions each morning. I had heard Elisabeth Elliot's message and genuinely desired to be obedient to the Master's voice. But now for the first time I realized what such obedience might cost me personally.

Unrealistic images of the missionary life underlined by a sense of adventure, noble thoughts, faraway exotic places, and fruitful ministry to the masses all collided with the clear picture of sacrifice that Helen Roseveare had just painted for us.

At the time the sacrifice seemed minor enough. I was a college sophomore with my life ahead of me. Singleness was a possibility but the thought of being single did not bother me at the moment. I was not in college looking for a husband and if God wanted to give me one, that was His business. But when I thought of my family, I had a problem. My parents, my brother, and my sisters were the ones who represented those I loved, and the family ties that I felt were strong. Being a missionary would mean a separation from loved ones, a separation of continents for long periods of time. This was a reality that I had not yet considered while singing praises and listening with rapt attention to challenging messages.

It is easy to sing God's praises and speak of sacrifice when we're sitting where we want to be. But when Christ calls us elsewhere and we're not ready to go, we tend to be reluctant little boys lingering on the piano bench.

With a very real sacrifice before me, I had to wonder if I could do this if God asked it of me. This was no longer a question generated by an enthusiastic crowd mentality; it was now a question between the Lord and me alone. I looked out of the window and talked it over with Him until I knew that I could not continue to sing praises at home if the Lord I loved was calling me to sing them elsewhere. That night began a habit of saying yes to the Lord not out of duty but out of love for Him; not because I wanted necessarily to do what He asked of me but simply because He was the one who asked.

Louis and I later had the privilege of talking with Dr. Roseveare in person. She was speaking again in the United States and happened to be at WEC's American headquarters at the same time we were. God had kept the vision for missions alive in both of our hearts ever since that Urbana

conference eleven years before. By this point Louis and I had been mar-
ried for seven years. Louis had finished all of his medical training, we had
both received a graduate degree in Bible at Columbia International University in preparation for missions, and now we were at WEC headquarters
with our three children as candidates preparing to go overseas.

Sitting at a table in the large paneled dining hall at headquarters, we
talked with Dr. Roseveare for several hours. She was interested in our
young family because Louis is a physician but also because we were on
our way to Chad, a country which she knew was not going to be an easy
field of service. I wondered what she was thinking as a retired missionary with all of her years of experience and her understanding of what
might lie ahead for this young doctor and his wife and three small children. Did we know what we were getting ourselves into? What lessons
would the Father have for us in the years ahead? Would we be able to
take all that He might give us and do all that He might require of us for
His sake?

At some point in the conversation, we told her how much her message had meant to us as students seeking God's will for our lives. It hadn't
been the usual missionary appeal. At that moment her questions stopped.
She smiled somewhat mischievously and told us with her wonderful
British accent, "I have decided that I must have the ministry of discouragement." She saw the look of surprise on our faces and went on to say,
"My job is to tell how hard it is and then if someone still goes, the Lord
has truly called them."

Louis and I looked at each other and then at our children who were
going so trustingly with us to Chad. We had certainly found life very
agreeable in the United States as a young family up to this point, and
Louis had recently been offered a position on the faculty of his residency
program. Were we really ready to give up such a life and future for a life
in Chad? But Dr. Roseveare's words rang true. Louis and I had already
asked the question and had received the answer we needed from the
Lord. We knew that we were truly called. The Lord had kept His

commitment to the world on our hearts throughout the early years of marriage and then had clearly told us during a weekend in the mountains that He wanted us to serve Him overseas. We knew that Christ had called us and that was enough. In response to His voice we were to go.

Jesus Our Example

Jesus never asks us to walk in a way that He hasn't Himself in some way already passed through. He is our example of obedience even when it comes with a price. We will never be able to imagine until we see Christ in the glory of heaven what it cost Him to obey the Father and leave behind that glory for earth. Paul ventures to describe this obedience in his letter to the Philippians:

> Your attitude should be the same as that of Christ Jesus: who, being in very nature God, did not consider equality with God something to be grasped, but made himself nothing, taking the very nature of a servant, being made in human likeness. And being found in appearance as a man, he humbled himself and became obedient to death—even death on a cross!
> —Philippians 2:5-8

J. I. Packer attempts to put more flesh on the truth of God becoming man in his book *Knowing God:*

> We see now what it meant for the Son of God to empty Himself and become poor. It meant a laying aside of glory (the real kenosis); a voluntary restraint of power; an acceptance of hardship, isolation, ill-treatment, malice, and misunderstanding; finally, a death that involved such agony—spiritual, even more than physical—that His mind nearly broke under the prospect of it. (See Luke 12:50, and the Gethsemane story.) It meant love

to the uttermost for unlovely men, who "through his poverty, might become rich." The Christmas message is that there is hope for a ruined humanity—hope of pardon, hope of peace with God, hope of glory—because at the Father's will Jesus Christ became poor, and was born in a stable so that thirty years later He might hang on a cross. It is the most wonderful message that the world has ever heard, or will hear.[2]

"At the Father's will." These words describe the heart of Christ while He walked among us on earth. Jesus was constantly thinking of His Father and never forgot that His goal while in this world was to do the Father's will. He reminded the disciples of this goal often in an effort to point them in the same direction.

When the disciples found Him at the well in Samaria, He had just finished having a life-giving conversation with a woman who had come to draw water from the well. Eternity had just been settled for her and for many more Samaritans after she returned to town to tell them of her conversation with Jesus. The disciples, not knowing this, found Jesus sitting alone at the well in the heat of the day and urged Him to eat. He told them He wasn't hungry and they wondered if somehow He had found food elsewhere. But Jesus was not filled with physical food; He was filled to satisfaction doing the will of His Father. "My food . . . is to do the will of him who sent me and to finish his work" (John 4:34), He told the disciples. "Open your eyes!" He urges them. "Look at the fields! They are ripe for harvest. Even now the reaper draws his wages, even now he harvests the crop for eternal life, so that the sower and the reaper may be glad together" (vv. 35–36).

Later, when a disgruntled crowd of disciples are having a hard time accepting His teaching, Jesus is not really concerned for their opinions of Him. He is more concerned that He is faithful to the Father: "For I have come down from heaven not to do my will but to do the will of him who sent me" (John 6:38).

The heart of the Son was always for the glory of the Father, and Jesus knew that He would bring glory to His Father through obedience. After His years of ministry on earth, He was able to say to the Father in prayer, "I have brought you glory on earth by completing the work you gave me to do" (John 17:4).

Nowhere is the heart of Jesus laid so bare as in the Garden of Gethsemane in the hours before He is betrayed and sentenced to death. Nowhere in Scripture is there a greater example of a life yielded wholly to the will of God. And nowhere else have I found greater comfort when I have felt the personal cost of what God was asking me to do for His sake. Jesus does not ask us to do hard things without knowing Himself what it means to count the cost. Gethsemane shows us that God understands even when we find it hard to say yes.

In the garden, Jesus knew what was coming and He was not looking forward to it. He also knew without a doubt that God could do anything, even stop the horror that He was about to allow His Son to experience. So in the anguish of the moment, using a term for *father* usually heard only from the lips of small children, the Son asked the Father to just this once give Him a reprieve from obedience. He prayed, "*Abba*, Father, . . . everything is possible for you. Take this cup from me" (Mark 14:36). Jesus' words are short and to the point: "Dad, You can do anything You want. Put a stop to this. Don't make Me do it."

We could understand if Jesus had ended the prayer with this request, but then we would not have the example of complete surrender that followed. Even with full knowledge of what was ahead and with His entire being crying out against having to go through with something He dreaded, Jesus had the glory of the Father on His heart and finished the prayer with the words, "Yet not what I will, but what you will."

In an earlier conversation with His disciples, Jesus prepared them for His leaving with these words: "You heard me say, 'I am going away and I am coming back to you.' If you loved me, you would be glad that I am going to the Father, for the Father is greater than I. I have told you now before it happens, so that when it does happen you will believe. I will not speak with you much longer, for the prince of the world is coming. He has no hold on me, *but the world must learn that I love the Father and that I do exactly what my Father has commanded me*" (John 14:28–31, emphasis mine). Jesus knew the Father intimately and loved Him deeply. Out of this relationship came wholehearted commitment to the Father's glory, wholehearted faith in the Father's ability, and wholehearted obedience to the Father's will.

There are three things that we can learn from Jesus' example in the garden. That we can be completely honest with Him when following Him seems incredibly, even sometimes unfairly, difficult. He can handle our honesty because He understands. He has been there. We also learn from Jesus' struggle in Gethsemane that we can ask in faith for whatever we want because God is able to do all things, but that if God's glory is truly on our hearts we are to submit in faith to whatever God wills. Complete honesty. Complete faith. Complete submission.

Peter's Mistake

Jesus is our example of complete surrender to God's will and we want to be like Him in all things, for "to this you were called, because Christ suffered for you, leaving you an example, that you should follow in his steps" (1 Peter 2:21). But the truth is, we tend to be more like Peter, who had to learn what obedience means.

When Jesus was in the Upper Room with His disciples celebrating the Passover Feast, He was quite literally the most powerful man on the earth at that moment. "The Father had put all things under his power" and He knew it (John 13:3). He also knew the glory that He had come from and He knew that He was returning to that glory. But knowing the power that was at His disposal, knowing His glorious roots, and knowing that He would soon be once again in the throne room of heaven, Jesus did an amazing thing. He took on the role of a servant. Not that of a high-ranking servant, like those who place food on the table, but the role of a common servant, the ones who stoop low and wash feet. He got up from the table where the meal was in the process of being served, took off his outer clothing, and wrapped a towel around His waist. He found a basin and poured water into it, then knelt before the other men in the room and began to wash their feet.

This was too much for Peter, who was watching Jesus move humbly from one disciple to the next. When Jesus came to him, Peter asked, "Lord, are you going to wash my feet?" Jesus saw his confusion and assured Peter that even though he did not understand what all of this meant now, he would understand it later. Peter still could not handle Jesus doing such a thing and said to Him, "No, you shall never wash my feet," but Jesus replied, "Unless I wash you, you have no part with me." I wonder how Jesus looked at Peter when He said these words? Did He look sorrowful that Peter once more was not getting the point? Did He smile briefly and think He was going to miss Peter's impetuous responses? Or did He speak with a firm no-nonsense shake of his head because of the seriousness of what was ahead? Whatever Peter heard in the Lord's voice or saw in His eyes, it caused him to say quickly, "Then, Lord, . . . not just my feet but my hands and my head as well!"

In this exchange between Peter and Jesus, Peter says in succession "Lord," then "No," then "Lord." It is either "no" or "Lord" but not the two together. Early in my Christian life I often heard the statement, "Christ is either Lord of all or not Lord at all." We cannot say "no" while saying "Lord" and we cannot say "Lord" while saying "no." If Christ is Lord of our lives, then walking a path of obedience means saying "yes" to whatever He asks us to do.

Obedience Leads to Joy

The path of obedience is not always easy, and you may well feel the cost of following Christ wholeheartedly. The cost for you may not be felt in the way we have felt it as missionaries, but Jesus will ask you to do some hard things if you are serious about following Him. In today's society, the cost may in some way be to your reputation among your friends, family, or colleagues. Very often you will be misunderstood because of your obedience to Christ.

The possibility of being misunderstood for our faith is a reality for Christians in the world today, and I must say that it helps to keep things in perspective. François Fénelon's commonsense advice in *The Royal Way of the Cross* is, "And let people take you for a fool; there is much truth in that." As long as we are free from concern for our reputation before others, we are free to be fully concerned with God's opinion of us.

Following the path of obedience will mean holding to biblical truth at the cost of your reputation among friends or colleagues who prefer that truth be relevant or nonexistent. Jesus will ask you to be honest when dishonesty might mean more profit for the business. He will ask you to remain sexually pure in both body and mind when there is no marriage on the horizon or when the sexual orientation you feel is not in line with His standards. He will ask you to be faithful in a marriage when love has grown stale or when someone else promises at the moment more excitement than your spouse. He may ask you to let go of things you would rather hold on to. He may ask you to deny yourself something you desire and that is possible for you but that does not further His purposes for your life. He may ask you to live more simply in order to honor Him more with your finances.

Your personal call to obedience may be less dramatic but nonetheless difficult. Choosing to let go of a grudge and being the first one to forgive. Stepping out of your comfort zone to lend a hand at a shelter for the homeless on a regular basis. Firmly booting out of your mind thoughts that are not honoring to God each time they try to settle in. Or simply placing a personal desire or anxiety at the foot of the cross and leaving it there in God's control. These sacrifices may seem little in the eyes of the world, but they are important to God. I have heard it said that a little thing is a little thing, but faithfulness in a little thing is a great thing.

Several years ago a young man I know was expecting a visitor for a few days. A female friend of his was passing through town and would need a place to stay while she was visiting. He naturally invited her to stay in his apartment for the few days. Since she was his friend and she knew no one else in town, the decision made sense to him and he thought nothing of it until his pastor, also a good friend, challenged this idea.

"Why not?" the young man asked in surprise. He knew very well what the pastor was concerned about and was irritated at the suggestion since he himself was a strong Christian and he and the young woman were definitely just good friends. Nothing at all was likely to happen and it was only for a weekend. Besides, he argued, who pays attention to things like this now? The pastor suggested that God pays attention to them still and challenged the young man to consider what the action, as innocent as it really was, would do for God's reputation, not to mention his own. His neighbors, knowing him as a Christian and a single man, might interpret the weekend in their own way regardless of the reality of the situation. "Keep away from even the appearance of evil" (1 Thess. 5:22) was a verse the young man had not thought much about. He agreed that if he truly cared for obedience to Christ it meant caring for God's glory in the eyes of others—even when he felt an action was not necessarily wrong. He found a place for his friend to stay for the weekend with a couple in the church. This was a little thing, a passing incident in a young man's life, but it required his obedience to God's way of thinking rather than his own. And because he truly desired to honor God in his life, he obeyed.

Christ does not ask these things of us to make life difficult or dull. He asks them because through them He will lead us into the deep joy and satisfaction that we will find only by seeking the higher things of His kingdom. "As the Father has loved me, so have I loved you," Jesus told His disciples and He tells us. "Now remain in my love. If you obey my commands, you will remain in my love, just as I have obeyed my Father's commands and remain in his love. *I have told you this so that my joy may be in you and that your joy may be complete*" (John 15:9–11, emphasis mine). Joy is the flip side of obedience and Jesus knows this. He calls us to obedience so that we can remain in His love and experience His joy.

"Religion as a dull habit is not that for which Christ lived and died," the Dutch priest Thomas à Kempis observed in the fifteenth century. His words hold true today. Obedience to Christ will not mean a life of dull habit. It actually makes of life an adventure as we follow our Lord in a way that goes against the grain of the world in which we live. My daughter, Elizabeth, has a T-shirt with the words "Why Be Normal?" dancing across the front. Following in obedience to Christ is definitely not the norm for today's world, but then, why settle for being part of the crowd? As we go against the grain of society by living in obedience to God's standards, we find that Christ leads us into greater things than we could ever have imagined for ourselves. We find, too, that along His path is a greater peace, greater joy, and greater satisfaction than we would have found walking in any other way.

I think back again to the message given by Helen Roseveare so many years ago. In the first few minutes of her message she had in her hands a large branch resplendent with leaves. As she spoke, all eyes were riveted to the branch as Dr. Roseveare slowly pulled each leaf from the branch, one by one, until it was completely stripped of the leaves and all that was left was a straight arrow, a useful and ready tool in her hands. Her point: the cost of obedience may seem great and sometimes senseless, like the stripping away of beautiful leaves that apparently ruined the beauty of the branch, until we see what God has in mind through the pruning: making our lives more effective, more useful, in His hands.

Choosing to walk in obedience does not mean that the path God leads us on will be smooth. There may well be thorns strewn along the path (remember Paul's "thorn in the flesh" that he desperately wanted God to take away but had to, in the end, be surrendered) or bends in the road that we are not prepared for and are hesitant to take. There may be times that it feels as if God is stripping away things that we value and would rather hold on to, like the beautiful green leaves of the branch that Dr. Roseveare held in her hand.

But if we have on our hearts the Father's glory, as Jesus did, and if we choose to walk in obedience to His will even when it costs us something, we will find that any path He chooses for us is deeply satisfying. God does not need to prove Himself to us, neither His love nor His wisdom in choices nor His faithfulness, but He will prove Himself over and over again. He will prove His faithfulness to every "yes, Lord" that we speak, and as we walk in the path of obedience we will find that it is also a path of joy.

Notes for the Journey

Whatever the particular call is, the particular sacrifice God asks you to make, the particular cross He wishes you to embrace, whatever the particular path He wants you to tread, will you rise up and say in your heart, "Yes, Lord, I accept it; I submit, I yield, I pledge myself to walk in that path, and to follow that Voice, and to trust Thee with the consequences"? Oh! But you say, "I don't know what He will want next." No, we none of us know that, but we know we shall be safe in His hands.[3]
—Catherine Booth

For Reflection

Obedience to God's will in our lives begins with obedience to His will as it is already revealed in the Bible. What do these verses have to say about obedience and our relationship with God?

- Luke 6:46
- John 14:15, 21–24
- John 15:9–10
- 1 John 2:3–6
- 1 John 5:3

In the book of Deuteronomy, the Israelites have finished their forty years of wandering in the desert and are on the verge of entering the Promised Land. Moses takes this moment to remind them of God's faithfulness and of His commandments. Throughout the recitation he reminds the Israelites (and us today) that God's commandments are for our good. Read the following verses from Deuteronomy and write what God says personally to you through them:

- Deuteronomy 2:7
- Deuteronomy 4:9, 39–40
- Deuteronomy 5:29, 32–33
- Deuteronomy 6:4–12
- Deuteronomy 7:9
- Deuteronomy 8:10–14

Suggestion

Ask God to reveal areas of your life where you are not being obedient to His biblical standards. Is there something He is asking you to do and you are hesitant? Is there something He is asking you not to do and you are unwilling to let go of it? Remember that God works His will in our lives for His glory and for our ultimate good. We will be most fully satisfied when we are in the center of His will. He only says no to something in order to say yes to His best for us.

An Inside Look: Growing in Obedience

By the time that we actually embarked on our missionary career, I had
become used to the idea of separation from my family. It was no longer
a problem for me since I had been away physically from the family circle
since college, with work and marriage taking me to other towns. By now
Louis and the children were the immediate family circle that mattered
most to my heart, and we would be together even on other continents.
We spent a year and a half in Belgium learning French and, for Louis,
tropical medicine, then we finally set foot on Chadian soil in September
1990. Scott was seven years old and Elizabeth and Susan were five at the
time.

God was gracious and provided a wonderful single woman, Cindy
Talley, who came to Chad with us to teach the children. Cindy with her
lovely smile and generous heart came for one year and fell in love with
Chad so that she ended up staying with us for two years. She became
like a sister to us. With Cindy teaching the children, I was free in the
mornings to learn Arabic alongside Louis and to concentrate on developing relationships with neighbors. After Cindy returned to the States,
there were two other young women, Jeanine Owens and Jennifer Brown,
who came as short-term missionaries to teach. They joined our family
circle and taught the children while having for themselves a mission
experience living in an African bush setting. With these helpers, I had
the best of both worlds as a missionary mother. My children were right
beside me and yet I had the free time to give outside of the home to
evangelism. Later, when no other short-term volunteers were in the pipe-
line, I homeschooled the children myself and thoroughly enjoyed the
concentrated time with them in our one-room classroom across the
sandy yard from our house.

This lasted for the first six years of our missionary career. Toward the
end of our second term in Chad we realized that our children were going
to need more than homeschooling in a remote African town, so we were

faced with the choice of returning to the United States after two terms on the field or sending our children to boarding school so we could continue in Chad. Suddenly the question of separation from family that had challenged a single college student looking out of a bus window came back to me, but this time it was much more personal and painful because I was now a mother and we were talking about my children.

Louis and I had to decide if we were going to continue in Chad as missionaries or return home to the United States for our children's education. Continuing in Chad, of course, meant that we would have to consider boarding school for the children and that would mean separation as a family. The decision was very hard, but in our hearts we knew that it was ultimately not our choice to make. It was a question of what God wanted us to do. We prayed for a year and in that time the Lord made it clear that our work in Chad was not yet finished. We agreed to continue on the field. Once the decision was made, His peace flooded our hearts and the children's excitement at the prospect of going to a boarding school helped tremendously.

I still remember the sadness, though, that I felt one day when another missionary who knew we were struggling over this issue asked what we had decided to do.

"We believe that we're supposed to stay on in Chad," I told her.

"Oh, then," she replied quite innocently, "you've chosen between the children and ministry."

My face must have registered the shock of her words, but even if she missed my expression, she certainly caught the protest in my response. "No, it's not that at all. If it was a choice between ministry or children, we could choose to minister anywhere and still be together as a family. It was a choice between obedience and disobedience."

When you know the thing God is asking of you, there are only two choices: to obey or to disobey. We either forget for the moment that He is Lord of our lives, like Peter in the Upper Room, and say no to what He has clearly asked us to do, or we say, "Yes, Lord, not my will but Thy will be done." At the root of all our choices, if we are sincere in following Christ, is whether or not we want to honor Him more than anything else in our lives, more than even our own desires. "Discipleship," Dietrich Bonhoeffer wrote, "never consists in this or that specific action: it is always a decision, either for or against Christ."[4] And so it was for Louis and myself at this point of decision. We could not say no to His clear direction and still claim He was Lord of our lives.

We returned to Chad for a third term in 1997, and the children began their boarding school experience at Black Forest Academy in the southwestern corner of Germany. I am writing this chapter four years later, and we can look back now and see God's tremendous faithfulness over these years. We have been together with our children for the summer months, for Christmas and Easter breaks, and have reveled in these times of family togetherness; our children have thrived at Black Forest Academy; and the separations have always been harder on us as parents than on them. The cost of obedience is still felt keenly at times, though. One morning on the last day of a two-week vacation together, in response to a friend's long-standing request that I write an article about sending our children to boarding school, I wrote down my thoughts:

> I woke up this morning thinking, I don't want to be at this point. Not at the end of vacation. Not at the time to say good-bye . . . again.
>
> We have just spent a wonderful two weeks as a family: a cherished time of nonstop togetherness, laughter, hugs, and discussion. And today it ends for another three months. We will send the children back to boarding school and Louis and I will head back to a house that seems too quiet, too empty, after all the energy that has just left.
>
> Saying good-bye does not become easy just because we have done it before. Separation from our children so they can receive a good education while we continue our ministry in Chad is the

hardest thing God has asked of us yet. Sometimes, the ache of missing them is so great that I have to say to the Lord, "I wouldn't do this for anyone else but You."

And that is true. Only the Lord is worthy of such a sacrifice. I do not think He asks it of us lightly, either. He knows fully what such a sacrifice means. He was the Son who has separated from His beloved Father and thought of Him constantly. He sought to be near Him whenever, and however, He could—in the Father's house, alone with Him on a hillside, talking with Him in prayer.

Jesus knew, too, what it is like to be asked to do a hard thing, something He would have preferred not to experience (Thank You, Lord, for Your honesty in Gethsemane). He knew the keenest pain of separation at the cross, when our sin placed on His shoulders blocked all access to the One He loved most. No, I do not believe He asks this of us lightly.

But it is true that He is worthy of our obedience. When the Lord made it clear that our work in Chad was not yet finished and that we should return for a third term, Louis and I knew that our children would need more from school than we could offer at home in a bush town. It was the hardest decision we have ever had to make and the bottom line was trust. I struggled with the Lord for nearly a year over this one. Surely He had given us children as a responsibility and never meant us to give that responsibility to someone else. My arguments were plenty. "Yes, Lord, I know that one day they will need to be on their own, independent of us. But not at twelve and fourteen years old! Never mind that others have done it far earlier and sent their children farther away for the sake of the gospel. We're talking about our family here and what is right for us."

The turning point came one day when I was praying for the children. I was using a guide to family prayer that my mother-in-law had recently sent to me. On this particular day, I was praying the words that followed the question, "Lord, what do You want for my children?" The prayer went along these lines:

"I release them to You so You can accomplish Your will in their lives."

(Pause … hmmmm)

"I will not try to relive my life through them. Keep me from binding them by my needs, wants, and ambitions for them."

(Longer pause, and a growing sense of uneasiness)

"Get me out of Your way so that You can work the life of Christ in them, and give them Your best."

(OK, Lord, enough! I surrender!)

I knew at that moment that I was praying for one thing, yet was really working hard for another. By digging in my heels over the issue of separation, I was in danger of working against what God wanted to do in the lives of my children. From this heavenly perspective, boarding school was not merely a solution to how we could remain on the field. It was the very thing God wanted for our children. It was the new arena in which He intended to shape their lives. As parents we had to trust Him in this—that He knew what He was doing with our children.

Letting go was the first and hardest step. Then we simply watched God's faithfulness unfold. How we came to send the children to Black Forest Academy while we work in Africa is a story in itself. But from the minute the decision was made, we have known it was right. The children love BFA and we are continually thankful they are in such a good place.

Still, it is not easy to say good-bye again. But it helps when I read a note like the one that our daughter Elizabeth slipped into my hand before our last good-bye, saying, "Mom, read this when you're on your way home." I remember that as we were driving away from them and the ache was very strong in my heart, I pulled the flowered stationery she had written on from its matching envelope and read the following words that I will always cherish:

Dearest Mom and Dad,

Last year at the beginning of school, you said, "I feel as if I am giving away my treasures." Well, I just wanted to remind you, as an encouragement, that for one thing, as a baby you gave our lives to the Lord, as well as each one of us having at one point given up our own lives again to God . . . and my mind, soul, spirit, body. Therefore we are not yours to give! And you know God won't give us up! Have a safe trip home.

Elizabeth

So now why am I crying as I remember her words? Because it does indeed look as if God knows what He is doing.

When I survey the wondrous cross,
On which the Prince of glory died,
My richest gain I count but loss,
And pour contempt on all my pride.

Forbid it, Lord, that I should boast,
Save in the death of Christ my God;
All the vain things that charm me most,
I sacrifice them to His blood.

See, from His head, His hands, His feet,
Sorrow and love flow mingled down;
Did e'er such love and sorrow meet,
Or thorns compose so rich a crown?

Were the whole realm of nature mine,
That were a present far too small;
Love so amazing, so divine,
Demands my soul, my life, my all.

—Isaac Watts

Eleven

A Path of Glory

All Christian thinking must not begin with man,
but with God.
—William Temple

Not to us, O LORD, not to us
but to your name be the glory,
because of your love and faithfulness.
—Psalm 115:1

The image of life as a journey is not by any means a new one. John
Bunyan immortalized this image in his book, *Pilgrim's Progress.*
In fact, the complete title of Bunyan's allegory of the Christian faith is
The Pilgrim's Progress from This World to That Which Is to Come. The
title is quite a mouthful, but it conveys one message of the seventeenth-
century pastor who wrote it: that the world we now live in is not all there
is. A greater world awaits us, one that lasts for eternity; and life in this
world is only a progressive journey or pilgrimage toward the true life
that awaits us in heaven. Perhaps Bunyan was recalling the words of
Psalm 84 while he sat in prison writing the book that was to become a
spiritual classic. "Blessed are those whose strength is in you, who have
set their hearts on pilgrimage," the psalmist writes (Ps. 84:5). I like even
better how the translation reads in the *New American Standard Bible.* A
pilgrim, according to this version, is one "in whose heart are the highways to Zion!"

When we begin our life with Christ, God puts in our hearts a pathway toward our true home in heaven. And once eternity is planted in our hearts, we are never again the same. The Latin phrase *carpe diem,* which means "seize the day" and which changed the lives of a group of students at an elite high school in the movie *Dead Poet's Society,* is no longer enough for the Christian. Our life motto becomes "seize eternity." Why settle for just a day when we can have eternity?

A pilgrim heart is unlimited in its scope. It is also undivided in its loyalty. We are never again the same because God has put within us a heart that beats for Him, a heart that longs to know Him and desires to be obedient to His commands:

> I will give them an undivided heart and put a new spirit in them; I will remove from them their heart of stone and give them a heart of flesh. Then they will follow my decrees and be careful to keep my laws. They will be my people, and I will be their God.
>
> —Ezekiel 11:19–20

> I will give them a heart to know me, that I am the LORD. They will be my people, and I will be their God, for they will return to me with all their heart.
>
> —Jeremiah 24:7

When we have this heart for God, He responds with His own heart for us:

> I will give them singleness of heart and action, so that they will always fear me for their own good and the good of their children after them. I will make an everlasting covenant with them: I will never stop doing good to them, and I will inspire them to fear me, so that they will never turn away from me. I will rejoice

in doing them good and will assuredly plant them in this land
with all my heart and soul.

—Jeremiah 32:39–41

We have eternity planted in our hearts. We have the all-powerful, all-wise, all-loving God calling us His people and desiring to do us good. Why is it, then, that so many Christians still live dissatisfied and unfulfilled lives?

We know that life on earth is not all there is, that heaven awaits us and that one day we will be there. We sing about it, we hear it preached, and we read about it in the Bible. We know, too, that God calls us to take our eyes off of the world so that we can see Him more fully and experience the good He desires for us. We are reminded of this every Sunday from the pulpit. We know all of this, yet somehow we still live entrenched in the world around us and, once we have exited the church door on Sunday morning, very often look no different from the other dissatisfied, unfulfilled people walking around on the earth.

Something is wrong with this picture, but we cannot quite figure it out. What is the problem?

There is an old saying that what is in the well must come out. There are wells throughout the northern region of Chad. Some produce wonderfully clear water and others produce murky water. All of the wells look much the same above ground, but what counts for a thirsty Chadian is not how a well looks on the surface but what lies within. No matter how reliable a well may look, if it is filled with murky water, only murky water will be drawn out.

The same is true for our own lives. What is in the well must come out; therefore, what we are internally inevitably influences our external actions and choices in life. The well of our spirit is constantly being filled by what we see and hear. What we allow to fill the well will eventually come out in our words, our thoughts, our actions, our reactions, our priorities, our ambitions, and our choices. If the well of our spirit is being filled with the things of God, then what is of God will come out. If the well is filled with the things of the world, then what is of the world will come out.

Perhaps that is part of the problem. Even as Christians our spirits are more easily filled up with the world than with God because we hear and see more messages from the world around us than we do from church. While the biblical message of life's journey comes during a few hours on a Sunday morning and perhaps several more hours on another night of the week, the world's message of where we should be heading comes seven days a week.

The world's version of life's journey is everywhere. Secular books and articles on journeys toward wholeness or self-realization flood the market. Their target is a dissatisfied and constantly searching society. Their message is that self-fulfillment is found in having what we want and in doing what we want. Publicity and the media reinforce this message loudly through radio, television, and now cyberspace. Advertising campaigns would have us really believe that we need their products to be happy, healthy, and beautiful. The business world would have us really work as if financial prosperity is the key to happiness. Bumper stickers would have us really believe that the man who dies with the most toys wins. Slogans would really have us think that we can never be too rich or too thin. The media is everywhere, and we cannot help but listen to its message. Before we even realize what is happening, we buy into the world's foundational message that life is all about us fulfilling our needs.

One result of buying into the world's message is a life lived by the words "If I can only just . . . " Spoken or unspoken, these words lead to chronically dissatisfied lives. "Give a man everything he wants and at that moment everything will not be enough," were the insightful words of Immanuel Kant. How true. "If I can only just be thin, I'll be happy," we say. "If I can only just get this promotion, I'll feel successful." "If I can only just make this much more money a year, I'll be satisfied." "If I can only have that bigger house, I'll stop complaining."

There is, of course, nothing wrong with being successful in what we do or even with wanting to be successful. There is nothing wrong with having goals or desires, and there is certainly nothing wrong with being healthy and taking care of ourselves. A successful use of talents and skills is deeply satisfying, and goals give needed direction for planning. Kept in the right perspective, material possessions give pleasure and help us enjoy life. The problem comes when we make the success we desire or the possession we seek into something we must have in order to be happy and, in pursuing them, lose sight of the things that really matter and that truly satisfy: the things of God.

Pastor and author Frederick Buechner writes in his book *The Magnificent Defeat,* "Power, success, happiness, as the world knows them, are his who will fight for them hard enough, but peace, love, joy, are only from God."[1] When we allow the well of our spirit to be filled with the world's message of what brings happiness (the world's version of joy), we will end up spending our lives pursuing and even fighting yet never being satisfied. There will always be something that we do not yet have, and so we will never have enough. We are taken on a ride of perpetual unrest that ultimately leads nowhere.

A Disoriented Worldview

The world wants to take us on its own journey and if we go along for the ride, we may well end up like the passengers on an ill-fated trip through the desert of northern Chad. The harshest terrain for traveling in Chad is that of the Sahara desert in the far north. For vast distances there are no roads and no landmarks to aim for, just hundreds of miles of an endless sea of sand dunes. Several years ago a huge Chadian transport truck, piled high not only with goods from Libya but with hundreds of passengers perched high on top in the typical fashion of Chadian "public transport," attempted to cross the desert. A few days into the journey the driver became disoriented and lost his sense of direction.

He wandered around in circles in the midst of the hot sand dunes until eventually the truck ran out of fuel and stopped. The passengers had brought enough water to last for a week in the desert but no longer. Tragically, one by one all 187 passengers died of thirst.

The Chadian driver lost his way in the desert because he had lost sight of the proper direction. The passengers had carefully calculated the amount of water they would need for the journey until they reached their destination, but they were trapped on a truck that was going around in circles. The world is a driver that has lost its sense of direction. That direction was lost in the garden when Eve reached for the apple because she turned her heart from God to herself and led Adam to do the same. Eventually the world will run out of fuel and stop altogether. If we are not careful, we can find ourselves—even as Christians—riding on the wrong truck with a disoriented driver who is taking us nowhere.

The danger of becoming disoriented on the journey is real. For Christians, the danger comes when even our faith is shaped by the message of the world around us. How does this happen? Louis has an interesting way to present the problem that he often shares with churches when he is invited to speak.

If one were to diagram the world's message, Louis suggests, it would look like this: **World = me ➡ my needs.** And it would be understood like this: *the world is about me meeting my needs.*

As Christians we would look at this diagram, note the secular world's obvious focus on self, and claim emphatically that this is a wrong model to live by. But unfortunately this same self-focus has crept into the church as well. Although in the church we clothe this thinking in spiritual garb, it is still secular in its focus. I must admit that sometimes when I hear Christians in churches today speak of their spiritual journeys I wonder what they really mean. And when I see some of the titles on the shelves in Christian bookstores, I wonder what the focus really is. The words and titles suggest more the self-oriented focus of the secular media rather than the God-oriented focus of a follower of Christ.

This is not always the fault of the individual. A distorted gospel message from the outset may have planted the seed of a disoriented life focus. The faulty gospel presentation often looks like the following or some version of it: "Are you lacking peace, contentment, security in your life? Is life not working out for you? Do you have needs that are not being met; needs of intimacy, affirmation, or fulfillment? Then there is a block; a problem."

In this gospel message, the secular sentence diagram becomes a Christianized one: **World = Me ➡ | | ➡ my needs.** The underlying message is understood like this: *the world is about me meeting my needs and there is a block to this goal.* No gospel presentation would state the message this way outright, of course, but the wording is still based on the world's model, only it is now clothed in Christian garb. The message continues: "There is a problem in your life, and there is an answer to the problem. Jesus can meet your needs and He will do so if you only let Him."

Now the message is complete and a disoriented Christian worldview is born. The old diagram in its Christian version looks like this: **World = Me ➡ Jesus ➡ My needs.** And is understood like this: *the world is about me meeting my needs through Jesus.*

You may well wonder what is so wrong with this diagram because there is truth in it. Christ alone satisfies our needs and we are to look to Him and not anywhere else. God has created us for Himself, so there is indeed a God-shaped void in our lives that only God Himself can fill. This is a truth we are to live by, and Christ's ability to meet our deepest needs is part of our message. The problem is not with responding to this truth and asking Christ to satisfy my needs but with the assumption that surrounds this truth, an assumption that, unless changed, keeps me trapped in a secular worldview. The gospel presented in this way assumes that the world centers on me and my needs, and that I need to satisfy those needs. Thankfully, after responding to the Good News of Christ, I can now say that I have found the way to do this—through Jesus. But with such a starting point, life is still all about me. My life in Christ begins not with my living for Him but with Him living for me.

The truth of Christ is real but the worldview is still secular. This Christianized worldly view still begins with me and ends with me and somehow Jesus is sandwiched in the middle. Working from the wrong model in our faith gives us the wrong focus for our Christian life. It may make us Christians, but it keeps us in a secular worldview. By beginning my journey from this starting point, I am already disoriented and in danger of losing my way on the path.

Problems with Jesus in the Middle

There are some obvious problems with living by this disoriented Christian worldview. One major problem is theological. The Bible makes it clear that the world does not begin with us or end with us. The very first words of Scripture, Genesis 1:1, are "In the beginning *God* . . ." At this point we aren't even in the picture. In the last book of the Bible, God, now in the form of the risen and supreme Christ, says, "I am the Alpha and the Omega, the First and the Last, *the Beginning and the End*" (Rev. 22:13, emphasis mine). We are in the picture by now but we are not the ones on the throne. We have fallen on our faces before God in worship.

A biblical focus does not begin with us or end with us but begins with God and ends with God.

There is also a practical problem with the "me and my needs" approach to life. If the world is all about me meeting my needs through Jesus, then what happens when life becomes harder rather than easier because I am now a Christian? What happens when I am ridiculed because of Christian principles? What happens when I still feel lonely at times or when I struggle with temptation because of a commitment to living by Christ's standards of purity? Being a Christian is not a guarantee of an easy life. In fact, it may well carry more of a guarantee that in some areas life will be harder.

This is certainly the case for our Chadian brothers and sisters in Christ who have come out of Islam. They suffer much because of their identification with Christ. One of the first men to give his life to Christ in northern Chad, Ahmat Djibrine, lost his workshop where he repaired radios for a living because his uncle refused to rent the building to him after his conversion to Christianity. As the leader of the small group of Muslim background believers in our town, Ahmat regularly has his life threatened by overzealous Muslim teachers. Other young men in the group have experienced similar problems because of their commitment to Christ. Abdel Nabi lost his inherited property through the local Islamic court system. Mahamat was locked in a small building by his family until he agreed to recite the Islamic creed. Abakar and Djimi were imprisoned and beaten after their public baptism. For any of these courageous men, if their choices to follow Christ were based on gaining a satisfying life in the world's eyes, then they would quickly have to question their decision.

The same is true for any of us in the church, even when we are not persecuted for our faith. Fairly quickly we realize that becoming a Christian does not necessarily make life easier or solve all of our problems. If we came to Christ with the underlying assumption that our needs are what life is all about and these needs are not met as expected, what is the solution?

There are two possibilities. One is to give up on Jesus and toss Him out of the picture. Christianity is tried and found wanting and so is abandoned. Because Christianity has not worked in whatever way we were hoping it would work for us, we leave it altogether and try something else. A different religion, transcendental meditation, yoga, or some other life philosophy is next on the list. There are many people who do just this and spend their lives in a continual search for fulfillment because they equate satisfaction with a trouble-free life. They ride on a truck that goes around in circles, getting thirstier and thirstier until the truck stops and there is nothing left on board to sustain life.

The other solution is more subtle and therefore a less recognized result of this disoriented worldview: keep Jesus in the picture because He does fulfill some needs but look elsewhere to satisfy the ones that are unmet. Because Christianity is still part of the picture, we fail to see how we are missing the mark. Many sincere people who fill the pews of churches are living this way, with a faith in Christ but still trying to meet their needs in other ways: for affirmation through success in one's career, for security through a bigger bank account, for happiness through more possessions and bigger closets, for fulfillment through relationships.

Our pastor and good friend Frank Venable calls living this way a "Jesus plus" faith. We look to Jesus plus career or Jesus plus marriage or Jesus plus money in the bank to bring fulfillment in life. Jesus is in our life, true, but He is placed alongside all of the other priorities competing for our attention. Without a clear sense of orientation toward Christ alone, we pursue them all and end up never really being satisfied, not even with our faith.

"Satisfy us in the morning with your unfailing love, that we may sing for joy and be glad all our days" (Ps. 90:14). The psalmist has the right idea. He looks to God for satisfaction at the beginning of each day in order to have gladness and joy in all of his days. Whenever my life in Christ is far from glad and joyous, then I usually am looking in the wrong direction for satisfaction. I have begun to live from the wrong model of what life is ultimately all about and need to reorient myself in the right direction.

Keeping on Track

What is the correct model for a truly Christian worldview? We have already seen that a biblical model begins with God and ends with God. But there is more. In Ezekiel 36:22 God says to His chosen people, "It is not for your sake ... that I am going to do these things, but for the sake of my holy name." In Habakkuk, God gives us a glimpse of His ultimate goal that one day "the earth will be filled with the knowledge of the glory of the LORD, as the waters cover the sea" (Hab. 2:14). The book of Revelation prophesies the fulfillment of this goal:

> Great and marvelous are your deeds,
> Lord God Almighty.
> Just and true are your ways,
> King of the ages.
> Who will not fear you, O Lord,
> and bring glory to your name?
> For you alone are holy.
> All nations will come
> and worship before you,
> For your righteous acts have been revealed.
> —Revelation 15:3–4

A biblical model does not end with God, period, but with God's glory. Therefore, a diagram of the true Christian worldview looks like this: **World = God ➡ His Glory.**

And it is understood like this: *the world is about God working for His glory.* As a Christian who wants to live with the correct worldview, I need to say at the outset of my journey of faith: life is not about me meeting my needs through Jesus but about God working for His glory and I am the one who must fit into the equation.

The Bible is also clear about how I fit in:

> Bring my sons from afar
> and my daughters from the ends of the earth—
> everyone who is called by my name,
> whom I created for my glory,
> whom I formed and made.
> —Isaiah 43:6–7

> In him we were also chosen, . . . in order that we, who were the
> first to hope in Christ, might be for the praise of his glory.
> —Ephesians 1:11–12

> So whether you eat or drink or whatever you do, do it all for the
> glory of God.
> —1 Corinthians 10:31

Most of us become Christians in the first place because we have felt needs and have found that only Christ can meet them, but we are not to live our life of faith by that model. My goal as a Christian is not to live to meet my needs but to live for the glory of God. My model for life is to be God working for His glory through me.

Does this mean that my needs are not important to God or that in order to be a good Christian I must ignore them? Not at all. Our needs come with the creation package and God knows this, since He created us with these needs. And He does mean for us to be satisfied in life. That is why God looks from heaven on all of our frantic pursuits and says, "Why spend money on what is not bread, and your labor on what does not satisfy? Listen to me, . . . and your soul will delight in the richest of fare" (Isa. 55:2). He knows something that we have lost sight of since the garden—*that we will find ultimate satisfaction only in that which is ultimately satisfying—God Himself.*

The world begins with God and ends with God, and in His love He has created us to be part of His world. All of history is heading towards one goal "to be put into effect when the times will have reached their fulfillment—to bring all things in heaven and on earth together under one head, even Christ" (Eph. 1:10). When this happens, in the words of Habakkuk, the world "will be filled with the knowledge of the glory of the LORD, as the waters cover the sea." God's ultimate goal is His glory in the world through Christ, and He has created us to live in the meantime for the praise of His glory.

There is great freedom in living by God's model. Living for His glory releases us from the chronic dissatisfaction and insecurity that comes from living for self. When we have His glory on our hearts, then we are not concerned with our own glory and no longer need to conform to the world's images of success and beauty to feel good about ourselves or to show who we are to those around us. Neither does it matter if someone else's ministry is more recognized or their church is filled with more people. What matters is that the kingdom of God is advancing. Living for God's glory above our own frees us from jealousy and pride. It frees us from restless pursuits so that we can finally find the satisfaction that our hearts truly long for, the deep soul satisfaction that only comes from God Himself and that He longs to give.

Patience in the Process

After being challenged to have a correct worldview of life centering on God's glory and not our needs, you may easily think, as I have at different points along the way: "There is so much of the world around me and in me . . . how can I ever change? How can I hope to have a heart and mind devoted as fully as they should be to God's glory?" Take heart in the title of Bunyan's book that reminds us that the Christian life is progressive. It is true that we are not where we should be in our faith, but we are on our way. My imperfections and weaknesses are too obvious for me to ignore, so I am always aware that I'm not what I should be before God, but I rest in the fact that, by God's grace and enabling power, I am *becoming* what I should be. Becoming what God wants me to be for His glory is a process and it takes time. Life as a journey is just that: a life in process.

Amy Carmichael wrote encouraging words for us to remember as we walk this path of "becoming." Reflecting on the description of God as "a refiner and purifier of silver" from Malachi 3:3, she thought of a visit to the village goldsmith who lived near the Dohnavur mission: "This picture of the Refiner is straight from Eastern life. The Eastern goldsmith sits on the floor by his crucible. For me, at least, it was not hard to know why the Heavenly Refiner had to sit so long. The heart knows its own dross. Blessed be the love that never wearies, never gives up hope that even in such poor metal He may at last see the reflection of His face. 'How do you know when it is purified?' we asked our village goldsmith. 'When I can see my face in it,' he answered."[2]

We can take heart for the journey. God never wearies of us and He never gives up hope that we will be changed. The goldsmith did not stop working until he saw the reflection of his face in the metal, and God will never stop working in us until He can see His image in us.

> And we, who with unveiled faces all reflect the Lord's glory, are being transformed into his likeness with ever-increasing glory, which comes from the Lord, who is the Spirit.
>   —2 Corinthians 3:18

> Being confident of this, that he who began a good work in you will carry it on to completion until the day of Christ Jesus.
>   —Philippians 1:6

If you truly long to live for God's glory, then that longing is enough for Him to work with. He will take your heart's desire and work it into your life. I have always been encouraged by the fact the Christian life is not all up to me. Thankfully! The Master Refiner is at work in me and He is making me into a vessel that lives for the praise of His glory. Ask Him continually to purify your heart and make it wholly His. Do your part to pay attention to His message more than to the message of the world and to fill up the well of your spirit with His truths. Do your part to be obedient to what He tells you and to follow where He leads you. Then know that God will do His part to work His glory in you.

Notes for the Journey

The gods we worship write their names on our faces, be sure of that. And a man will worship something—have no doubt about that either. He may think that his tribute is paid in secret in the dark recesses of his heart—but it will out. That which dominates will determine his life and character. Therefore, it behooves us to be careful what we worship, for what we are worshipping we are becoming.[3]

—Ralph Waldo Emerson

For Reflection

How we speak often reveals what is in the well of our heart and mind. Listen to your "God-speech" to determine the worldview model you are living by:

- Do you speak only of your needs and how you want God to meet them or also of a desire for God to use you and work in you for His glory?
- What do you say when God does not answer your prayers in the way or timing you want Him to answer them? When things are not working out as you had hoped in your life? When doing what He has asked you to do actually adds difficulties rather than erases them from your life?

Listen to your "if onlys" to determine what you are looking to for satisfaction in life:

- Is there anything or anyone in your life that holds the place of honor that only God should occupy? Such as something you already have that occupies your thoughts and energies more than it should? Or something that you do not yet have that is causing dissatisfaction with God, with yourself, or with others around you such as a spouse or child or friend because you don't have it?

- How would you fill in this blank? "If I can only have_____, I would be happy."

- Mentally take this "idol" off the throne and submit it to God. Leave the space on the throne of your heart for God alone.

What do these verses say about God's glory?

- Exodus 20:3–6
- Exodus 34:14
- Isaiah 42:8
- Isaiah 48:11
- Romans 1:18–25
- Ephesians 1:11–14

About Jesus and God's glory?

- Matthew 16:27
- Matthew 24:30–31
- Matthew 25:31
- John 1:14
- John 8:54–58 (Exod. 3:13–15)
- Philippians 2:9–11

About how we live for God's glory?

- Isaiah 43:7
- John 15:5–8

- Romans 4:20–21
- 2 Corinthians 4:13–18
- Philippians 1:9–11
- Colossians 3:1–17
- 1 Thessalonians 2:4–6
- 1 Peter 2:12

Suggestion

Is God's glory safe with you? True humility is acknowledging the gifts, abilities, and successes that we have, but at the end of the day knowing where they come from. Corrie ten Boom once said that during the day she gathered all of her compliments and honors like flowers, accepting them with grace and thanks from the givers, but at night she handed them all in a bouquet to the Lord. She knew that any personal achievements and good that others saw in her ultimately were because of God's work in her life. Following her example is a good way to acknowledge our strengths and achievements while keeping ourselves from pride. And God's glory is safe with us because we do not take for ourselves what ultimately belongs to Him.

While we are still on this earth we see only glimmers and cracks through the great wall which exists between this life and the next. What will it be when we shall see him face to face? The focus then will be far beyond any mere experience. It will be on God Himself.

—Amy Carmichael

Twelve

A Path That Leads Home

Our whole life is given us with the object of going boldly on
towards the heavenly home.
—François Fénelon

Even the sparrow has found a home,
and the swallow a nest for herself,
where she may have her young—
a place near your altar,
O LORD Almighty, my King and my God.
—Psalm 84:3

My husband and I have not yet owned our own home here on earth. We rented a house during Louis's years of medical school in Chapel Hill, North Carolina, and then again during his residency in Columbia, South Carolina. Because we knew that we would eventually live overseas for missionary service and did not want the hindrance of a house to sell holding us back when we were finally free to go, we always chose to rent instead of to buy. This means, of course, that we have no home of our own and whenever we return to the United States for a furlough year, as we have done three times now since the beginning of our missionary career, each time we must rent again. Since we have few personal possessions on this side of the Atlantic Ocean, any house we rent needs to be furnished and is done so graciously by the generous donations and labor of our church family.

I remember well the first time the Lord spoke to me of homes. It was in Atlanta, Georgia, in the summer of 1977. I was on the way back to North Carolina from my first mission experience, having just spent three weeks in Guatemala through what was at the time called Overseas Training Camp sponsored by InterVarsity Christian Fellowship. My initial view of Guatemala as we took a bus from the airport to the site of our training camp had been of cardboard houses strewn along a hillside that looked like the city garbage dump. And there were people, many people, living in these houses. I would never forget the picture of such a mass of humanity sprawled on a hillside in makeshift housing.

Part of the mission training involved spending a week with a bona fide missionary. I was assigned along with another student to a Wycliffe missionary who was working in an Indian village outside of Guatemala City. There was little we could actually do to help in the missionary's ministry since we had no knowledge of the language, but we eagerly set to work painting the inside walls of a house she had just rented in a village where she would soon live. The house that she soon hoped to call home was a two-room cement block building that hugged the edge of a jagged cliff and had the village dump as her back porch view.

Our missionary host would take us on walks through the village, along thin mud trails and up steep hills to visit with short, broad Indian women who welcomed us shyly into their homes. We sat low to the ground on benches inside each house and smiled until our jaws ached, having no idea what was being said in the rapid conversation going on between our host and her friends. There was hardly room for two visitors much less three in the rough wooden shacks, but we were always made to feel welcome.

I had enjoyed thoroughly those summer weeks in Guatemala and as a result felt more strongly than ever the pull of serving God in missions. But now I was back in the United States, in the big city of Atlanta, in the house of a friend whom I had decided to visit on the way back to North Carolina. My friend's house was large and spacious, as were all of the

houses I could not help noticing during the two days we were together. If
I had come directly to Atlanta from North Carolina, I would hardly have
paid attention to my surroundings, but I had just come from a small
village in a poor country. I could not stop looking with great interest at
the houses that surrounded me now. They were beautiful homes typical
of the South's gracious living. They were just the kind of homes that I
dreamed of. Yet it was on the second day of looking at them that I realized that I could not get the images of one-room shacks with cardboard
walls and a two-room cement block building out of my mind. Somehow
I felt that I was not going to get one of these elegant, two-story Victorian
houses any time soon. I released a long, heavy sigh.

That night I was still feeling the sigh in my heart. At the time I was
reading through one psalm a day and that night my reading began with
Psalm 84, the psalm that soon became a favorite as I returned to it again
and again throughout the years that followed. My eyes ran over the opening words and then I stopped to read a second time the following:

> Even the sparrow has found a home,
>   and the swallow a nest for herself,
>   where she may have her young—
> a place near your altar,
>   O LORD Almighty, my King and my God.
> Blessed are those who dwell in your house;
>   they are ever praising you.
>   —Psalm 84:3–4

I knew that the Lord was speaking to me through this psalm. He understood the heart of a woman since He had created this heart with its
natural desire for a home. He spoke to my heart's desire that night these
words: "Even the sparrow has found a home. Even the swallow has a
place to build her nest and raise her young. Even for you, Susan, there
will be a home. It might be nothing but a thatch hut or a cement block

building, but it will be a home and it will be all you need. But that is not all I want you to know. More important than the external home you live in is the internal home. Look where the sparrows find their home and the swallows build their nest. Near Me."

I looked up from my comfortable bed in the home of my friend and finally saw beyond the spacious homes of my dreams to what God was saying. I would have a home sometime and somewhere, yes, but more important, no matter where I lived and no matter what type of home my dwelling would be, whether thatch or mud-brick or two-story Victorian, my real dwelling place would always be with Him.

This assurance has proven true over the years. We have lived in some interesting dwelling places during our missionary career, ranging from a low-rent apartment in downtown Brussels, Belgium, while studying French to simple mud-brick and cement houses in Chad to rental housing of various kinds when we return for a furlough in the United States. What has also proven true is the centuries-old counsel of Catherine of Siena: "Make two homes for yourself, my daughter. One actual home and another spiritual home which you carry with you always."[1] When I have been diligent to maintain my spiritual home with the Lord, I have found contentment, no matter what the size or condition of my physical home. There are times, of course, that I still long for a permanent home in America and may well one day have it, but looking back on our years as missionary nomads, I do not regret our lack of home ownership; I have had the privilege of finding my true home here on earth in Christ.

Home Is Where the Heart Is

We are to have two dwelling places while here on earth. Our earthly home and our spiritual home that we carry with us always. There is another idea of home that is part of our pilgrimage on earth and that, of course, is looking to our heavenly home. As pilgrims, we know that we are just passing through this world on the way to our true home in heaven.

We are not to be entrenched in the world, but are to live with minds and hearts devoted to Christ, living our lives on earth not for self-glory but for His glory. This idea is expressed wonderfully in the words of Thomas Watson: "The world is a but a great inn, where we are to stay a night or two, and be gone; what madness it is so to set our heart upon our inn, as to forget our home."

Heaven as our true home is another thread that has run throughout this book. I began our look at life as a journey with the description of a road that we had to travel in Chad in order to reach our home in Adre. We never asked ourselves the question "Is it worth it?" when we experienced the difficulties of the road, because of where the road led us. The same goes for the path God leads us on toward our heavenly home. When we encounter difficulties along the way, the question to ask is not "Is it worth it?" but "Is He worthy?" And the answer to that question is always yes. The road to home for the Christian is a road that leads us to the final ultimate pilgrim's encounter with God. What matters about home in this sense is not so much the place, although heaven is real, but who lives there.

Our children know this in a way that I can never fully understand. They are very much Third Culture Kids (TCK), that is, children who live in a culture different from where they were born. If they live overseas for most of their lives, TCKs do not identify with their birth country and as much as they might adapt, they will never truly be citizens of their host country. Not fully identifying with their birth culture or with the culture of their host country, TCKs become a blend of the cultures where they have lived. Missionary children are not the only Third Culture Kids in the world. Children of parents who live overseas for any length of time, whether it be for military or embassy or business purposes, all know what it feels like to wonder where "home" is.

If my own ideas of home are a little skewed, then it is more so for our three children. The idea of heading home for them brings about a mixed reaction. When they were little and we lived in Adre for three years at a time, home meant at the time our large mud-brick house and a yard that was to them the biggest sandbox in the world. But each time we prepared for a furlough year and Louis and I talked about going home, they were not quite sure what to think.

What does home mean to them? They were born in the United States but have lived all of their lives overseas. Although they have American passports, because of their years spent in Africa and Europe, they are far from American in their thinking. They not only have a blend of English, French, Arabic, and German in their vocabulary, but they have a blend of African, European, and American cultures in their personalities. Such a life experience has its advantages, which are readily seen by our family and friends. But it does mean that when we return to the United States for a period of time, they do not feel completely at home.

We remember with amusement the first time we returned home after living overseas for an extended period. We had been in Belgium for a year and half and were returning home for a short period before heading overseas to Chad. Scott was only five years old and Susan and Elizabeth only three when they left the United States for Belgium, so they had no memories of any particular city or state or even language that they might claim as their own. On the international flight from Brussels to Atlanta, Susan who was then four years old, hurried back to me after a walk down the aisle with her father and exclaimed with wide eyes, "Mommy, they're all speaking English!" After just spending a full year in a French-speaking kindergarten along with her twin, Elizabeth, this was indeed a revelation that there could be a place in the world where English was the main language.

Soon after we arrived in the United States, we stopped at a service station in a small town to fill the car with gas. Scott hopped out of the car to stretch his energetic six-and-a-half-year-old body and the friendly young man at the gas pump asked him where he was from. Scott looked him square in the eyes and said proudly, "I'm from the United States of America." The young man looked so surprised at such an answer that we had to laugh. He probably wondered if he'd missed a national holiday or something that would warrant such patriotism. Scott had just spent seven months at a British school in Brussels and the man may well have wondered at the decidedly British accent this young patriot used when he spoke. We eventually explained to him that we had just returned from living overseas and our children knew only that they were from America because that's what we had been telling them for the past few weeks.

Today, at eighteen and sixteen years old, they are more sophisticated in their responses but it still is not an easy question for them to answer. "So, where are you from?" a high school student asks our daughters at a church-sponsored mission week in Alabama. "Well," they say and take a deep breath, "we go to school in Germany but our parents work in Africa, and we were born in South Carolina, but when we're in the States we live in North Carolina." This marks them immediately in the eyes of their new friends as interesting but also different.

Their experience as Third Culture Kids may provide them with interesting conversation starters, but it has also provided them with what I think is the key to our understanding of what home is really all about and with it the key to an anticipation of our heavenly home.

"We're going home," we said to them once when it was time to head to America for another furlough year. "No, we're not," they said back to us. "So what, to you, is home?" we asked. They thought about it for a minute then replied, "Home is you."

When I heard their response, I thought, "Yes, that's it." Home is sometimes a place but home is also the people we love. Associating home with those we love is the key to my own heart being content in various homes in various places, because Christ, my spiritual home, is with me wherever I go. It is also the key to my thoughts about heading home to heaven.

I have to admit that most often in my thinking, heaven is more of a vague cloud in the by-and-by than a place I can relate to. Such thinking does not stir up within me great longings to be there. Not when everything I know, everything that is familiar and that I hold dear, is here in the sweet now-and-now. But there is a longing that God has placed within my heart that can only be satisfied by reaching heaven. That is the longing expressed by the psalmist in Psalm 84, the longing to be near Him. "They go from strength to strength, till each appears before God in Zion" (Ps. 84:7). The pilgrim makes his way toward the temple in Jerusalem, but his longing is not so much for the temple as for God who dwells there. Heaven, as I said earlier, is the ultimate pilgrim's goal of an encounter with God.

The Journey's End

Peter wrote in his first letter to the believers who were scattered throughout Asia, "Though you have not seen him, you love him; and even though you do not see him now, you believe in him and are filled with an inexpressible and glorious joy" (1 Peter 1:8). Even though we have not seen Christ, we love Him because of what He has done for us on the cross. As we begin to walk in obedience where He leads us, we find that He is always there beside us, leading us on a path of His faithfulness and wisdom, of His goodness and love. Even though we never see Him physically as we go through life, our love for Him grows as He reveals Himself to us in a thousand and one faithful ways.

There will be one day, though, that I am at the end of my earthly journey. I have heard death called "graduation day" and in a sense it is. Graduation is not the end but the beginning of the life ahead for students and so, as Dietrich Bonhoeffer knew, physical death really is not the end but the beginning of life. And what is that life? That we will finally get to see Christ face-to-face and be with Him for eternity, this One we have walked with, laughed with, and cried with, this Lord we have known and loved for so long.

C. H. Spurgeon wrote, "There will be little else we shall want of heaven besides Jesus Christ. He will be our bread, our food, our beauty, and our glorious dress. The atmosphere of heaven will be Christ; everything in heaven will be Christ-like: yes, Christ is the heaven of His people."

This is what heaven means. This is worth the journey.

Notes for the Journey

> My life is ending, I know that well, but every day that is left me I feel how my earthly life is in touch with a new, infinite, unknown, but approaching life, the nearness of which sets my soul quivering with rapture, my mind glowing and my heart weeping with joy.[2]
>
> —Fyodor Dostoyevsky

For Reflection

"Make two homes for yourself, my daughter. One actual home and another spiritual home which you carry with you always." Take some time to think about Catherine of Siena's words in light of this question: Are you taking as much care of your spiritual home, that is, your relationship with God, as of your physical home?

What kind of spiritual home does God provide for us while we are on earth?

- Psalm 27:4–5
- Psalm 32:7
- Psalm 61:1–4
- Psalm 71:1–3
- Psalm 90:1–2
- Psalm 91:1–2
- Proverbs 18:10
- Matthew 7:24–27

What do these verses say about the heavenly home that awaits us?

- 2 Corinthians 5:1
- 1 Thessalonians 4:16–17
- 2 Peter 3:13
- Revelation 7:9
- Revelation 21:1–22:5
- Revelation 22:1–6

Conclusion

Reflections on Psalm 84 from a Wandering Pilgrim

I have enjoyed traveling together with you for a while on the journey of faith, and I hope that this book has provided some encouragement for you. May the Lord bless you as you travel onward, drawing nearer to Him here on earth, and as you travel upward, drawing nearer to your home with Him in heaven. We may never meet personally in this life, but one day we will be together for eternity. Who knows? We may sit down together under heaven's version of a shade tree and share our journeys and rejoice in God's faithfulness, saying without a doubt that it was all worth the journey because He is worthy.

Here are some final reflections for you from the psalm that I have come to know and love along the way. I leave them with you for final encouragement, along with a parting prayer that you will always have the heart of a pilgrim.

> How blessed is the man whose strength is in Thee,
> In whose heart are the highways to Zion!
> —Psalm 84:5 (NASB)

We are pilgrims all, wanderers on this earth making our way home to heaven. The moment we claimed the name *Christian,* we became pilgrims. For Christ put in our hearts a longing for His glory, and He set our feet on this "highway" toward home.

We each have the same destination, but not always the same paths to lead us there. We each have, rather, our own paths to follow, our own ministries to fulfill, our own lessons to learn, all carefully designed by the One who set us on the path and called us to go.

There are resting places along the way for the traveler, providing moments of refreshment and renewal. We stop to drink of the good words and enjoy the companionship of other pilgrims, to receive instructions and needed encouragement that send us on.

Very often the Lord who called us gives us traveling companions for the road, fellow pilgrims following the same route, perhaps sharing the same vision. Our roads converge, and we travel together, encouraging, challenging, sharpening, understanding, and enriching each other's lives. Then the roads diverge, paths separate. I am called to go this way, you are asked to go there or, perhaps, to remain. We clasp hands, cry a little, promise to pray . . . the pilgrimage goes on.

> Passing through the valley of Baca [Weeping] they make it a spring;
> The early rain also covers it with blessings.
> —Psalm 84:6 (NASB)

The way of the pilgrim is not always easy. Often his path is found to be less desirable than what he would have chosen for himself, certainly more difficult than he imagined possible when he first set out. It is possible that the traveler becomes weary of the path or looks longingly at the paths of others, which, from a distance, look easier, more desirable, or more exciting than his own. It is even possible that he questions if he is on the right path, if perhaps he misunderstood the directions.

But unless the pilgrim experiences the "valley of weeping," he will never learn the secret of making it a "place of blessings." The secret is simple, yet often slowly learned. The secret is found in two words: "Yes, Lord."

They go from strength to strength,
Every one of them appears before God in Zion.
—Psalm 84:7 (NASB)

With each "Yes, Lord," with every "Even this, Lord, if You ask it of me," the pilgrim is strengthened for the journey. He can even learn in time to cherish the difficulties of the path, for as he travels, his eyes are sharpened. He begins to see the difficulties for what they truly are and he begins to understand that they have come from the hands of a wise and loving Father who knows him well and who knows what he needs to reach home. He discovers, too, that the more he keeps his eye on the Father as he travels, the more joy there is no matter what the present circumstances of the path. Easy or hard, exciting or mundane, fruitful or as the buried seed, the promise holds true:

No good thing does He withhold from those who walk uprightly.
—Psalm 84:11 (NASB)

And so the pilgrim goes from strength to strength, walking, learning, changing, strengthened in heart and limb, proving true the triumphant cry of the pilgrim:

O Lord of hosts,
How blessed is the man who trusts in Thee!
—Psalm 84:12 (NASB)

Endnotes

Chapter 1: The One Way Home

1. W. E. Vine, *"akalouthe,"* in *Vine's Expository Dictionary of Old and New Testament Words* (Old Tappan, N.J.: Revell, 1981).
2. Ingrid Trobisch, *On Our Way Rejoicing!* (New York: Harper and Row, 1964).
3. Eugene Peterson, *A Long Obedience in the Same Direction: Discipleship for an Instant Society* (Downers Grove, Ill.: InterVarsity, 2000).
4. J. I. Packer, *Knowing God* (Downers Grove, Ill.: InterVarsity, 1973).

Chapter 2: Hearts on Pilgrimage

1. *Merriam-Webster's Dictionary* (New York: Simon and Schuster, 1974), s.v. "pilgrim."
2. The author and recipient of the *Epistle to Diognetus* are unknown. This second- or third-century letter provides insight to the doctrine and life of the church in its day.
3. William Temple, *Christianity and Social Order* (New York: Penguin, 1944).
4. François Fénelon, *The Royal Way of the Cross,* Modern English Version by Hal M. Helms (Brewster, Mass.: Paraclete, 1997).

Chapter 3: A Companion for the Path

1. François Fénelon, *The Royal Way of the Cross,* Modern English Version by Hal M. Helms (Brewster, Mass.: Paraclete, 1997).
2. Hannah Whitall Smith, *The Christian's Secret of a Happy Life* (Old Tappan, N.J.: Spire Books/Revell, 1942).
3. Fénelon, *The Royal Way of the Cross.*
4. J. I. Packer, *Knowing God* (Downers Grove, Ill.: InterVarsity, 1973).
5. Fénelon, *The Royal Way of the Cross.*

Chapter 4: A Focus for the Path

1. Brother Lawrence, *The Practice of the Presence of God* (ed. and par. Donald E. Demaray [Grand Rapids: Baker, 1975]), continues to be one of the most influential spiritual classics of all time.
2. Susan Scott Sutton, *A Quiet Center: A Woman's Guide to Resting in God's Presence* (Grand Rapids: Kregel, 1999).
3. Amy Carmichael, *Candles in the Dark* (Fort Washington, Pa.: Christian Literature Crusade, 1981).
4. Ibid.
5. Thomas Doolittle, "What Is Love to Christ," Fire and Ice: Puritan and Reformed Writings (http://www.puritansermons.com/reformed/dool1.htm) 26 November 2002.

Chapter 5: A Light for the Path

1. George MacDonald, *Diary of an Old Soul* (Minneapolis: Augsburg Fortress, 1944).
2. C. S. Lewis, *The Four Loves* (New York: Harcourt, Brace, Jovanovich, 1960).
3. Amy Carmichael, *Thou Givest ... They Gather* (Fort Washington, Pa.: Christian Literature Crusade, 1958).

Chapter 6: A Path of Faith

1. G. Campbell Morgan, *Searchlights from the Word* (Old Tappan, N.J.: Revell, 1977).
2. Amy Carmichael, *Rose from Brier* (Fort Washington, Pa.: Christian Literature Crusade, 1973).
3. Quoted in Carmichael, *Rose from Brier*, 110.
4. A. B. Simpson, *Christ in the Tabernacle* (Camp Hill, Pa.: Christian Publications, 1985).

Chapter 8: A Path of Hope

1. Amy Carmichael, *Toward Jerusalem* (Ft. Washington, Pa.: Christian Literature Crusade, 1961).
2. Charles Haddon Spurgeon (1834–1892) was a great English preacher who spoke with power and humor. In his day he was called the "prince of preachers" and was so popular that it was difficult to find a place large enough to seat the crowds who came to hear him. He preached for thirty years in the Metropolitan Tabernacle, which seated six thousand. His sermons are collected in over fifty volumes and are still highly valued today.
3. Madeleine L'Engle, *Two-Part Invention: The Story of a Marriage* (New York: Farrar, Straus, and Giroux, 1988).
4. Ibid.
5. F. B. Meyer (1847–1929) was an English pastor and popular convention speaker. He is known for his devotional studies on biblical characters. Among his well-known books are *The Shepherd's Psalm, Christ in Isaiah,* and *The Glorious Lord.*

Chapter 9: A Path of Praise

1. Amy Carmichael, *Thou Givest... They Gather* (Fort Washington, Pa.: Christian Literature Crusade, 1991).
2. William Law (1686–1761) was an influential English writer on the subjects of Christian ethics and mysticism. His most well-known works are *A Serious Call to a Devout and Holy Life, A Practical Treatise upon Christian Perfection, The Spirit of Love,* and *The Spirit of Prayer.*

Chapter 10: A Path of Obedience

1. A. W. Tozer, *Keys to the Deeper Life* (Grand Rapids: Zondervan, 1987).
2. J. I. Packer, *Knowing God* (Downers Grove, Ill.: InterVarsity, 1973).
3. Catherine Mumford Booth (1829–1890) was the wife of William Booth, the founder of the Salvation Army. The mother of eight children, a popular speaker, reformer, and evangelist in her own right, Catherine Booth is considered one of the most influential women in modern Christian history.
4. Dietrich Bonhoeffer, *The Cost of Discipleship* (New York: Simon and Schuster, 1959).

Chapter 11: A Path of Glory

1. Frederick Buechner, *The Magnificent Defeat* (New York: HarperCollins, 1966).
2. Amy Carmichael, *Rose from Brier* (Fort Washington, Pa.: Christian Literature Crusade, 1973).
3. Ralph Waldo Emerson (1803–1882) was an American essayist, critic, poet, and orator whose works stand among the classics of American literature.

Chapter 12: A Path That Leads Home

1. Catherine of Siena (1347–1380) was born in Florence, Italy, and entered the Dominican Order at the age of sixteen. Although she was nearly illiterate, she became a spiritual leader in the church of her day. She influenced many through her letters, which she dictated to others.

2. Fyodor Dostoyevsky (1821–1881) is one of the greatest writers in Russian literature. At the age of twenty-eight he was arrested for reading political books banned by the Russian government and was sentenced to exile and hard labor in Siberia. He went to Siberia as an atheistic socialist but emerged four years later as a Christian. His faith pervades many of his greatest works such as *Crime and Punishment, The Idiot,* and *The Brothers Karamazov.*